W. K. Clifford

A Flash of Summer

A Novel

W. K. Clifford

A Flash of Summer
A Novel

ISBN/EAN: 9783337029340

Printed in Europe, USA, Canada, Australia, Japan

Cover: Foto ©Thomas Meinert / pixelio.de

More available books at **www.hansebooks.com**

A FLASH OF SUMMER

A NOVEL

BY

MRS. W. K. CLIFFORD

AUTHOR OF LOVE LETTERS OF A WORLDLY WOMAN,
AUNT ANNE, ETC.

NEW YORK
D. APPLETON AND COMPANY
1894

A FLASH OF SUMMER.

CHAPTER I.

EVERYONE on Shooter's Hill had known Katherine Kerr by sight since she was six years old. She seemed to be always walking up or down the great Dover Road — that wonderful road that stretches from London, through New Cross and Lewisham, across Blackheath, over Shooter's Hill to Welling and Bexley, and away to the coast far beyond. Every morning she came out of the White House, that was hidden among the trees, at the corner of the little road that leads to Severndroog, and walked down the garden pathway with the beeches overhead, opened the iron gate and came out on to the high road.

Close to the gate was a well to which the
inhabitants went with their pails in days of
drought before the water company came to
help them.   Just below was the grey little
church, and opposite was the post-office, es-
tablished for many a long year at an unobtru-
sive general shop ; and next to the post-office
the Red Lion, with its wide quadrangle and
tea gardens that were almost rural.   To the
tea gardens, on Sunday nights, the soldiers
from Woolwich and the Government servants
from the Royal Military Academy brought
their sweethearts, and sat with them at little
wooden tables in trellis-made summer-houses,
drinking beer.   They grew jovial as the evening went on.   Katherine listened to their
snatches of song and the din of voices till
darkness fell, and perhaps faint in the distance the bugle-call was heard : then gradually the merriment was hushed, and two and
two, always a he and she, the Sunday crowds
went down the hill and turned to the right
towards the barracks.   The little road they

took was known as The Lane, and led to
Woolwich : at one corner of it was a stuffed-
bird shop, and on one side of the shop window were toys and story-books for children.
Katherine looked in at them now and then,
and hesitated before she spent a stray penny
on "Jack and the Beanstalk" or "Cinderella."
At the other corner were four houses standing
in a block, known as Ordnance Terrace. In
the garden of the first house there was a
peach-tree trained up against the stable : and
she used to see the flushed fruit among the
long narrow leaves in the late summer, and
think how good it would be to touch it with
her fingers. Lower down was a plantation to
which the Artillery men came in the morning
to exercise their horses, and the clatter of
hoofs, and the shrill bugle, and the rushing
among the trees made her wonder if it was
like a battlefield. Opposite, on the other side
of the main road, was a wide expanse of gorse
and blackberry bushes, the great trees of Severndroog and its ruined tower showing above

them on the left; and on the right, beyond
the Scrubs, as the tangle of bushes was called,
a narrow road that led to Eltham went across
the landscape, and far beyond it stretched the
open country, showing the Crystal Palace in
the distance.

In the morning, when she came out of the
gate—every morning of her life from six to
seventeen, save on Sundays and during the
brief holiday periods—Katherine turned to her
left and went down the hill, past the church
on one side and the inn on the other, past the
stuffed-bird shop and The Lane that led to
Woolwich, and the four houses and the plantation and the Scrubs. Then she came to where
four roads met, or, rather, two branched off,
right and left, the one on the left to Eltham
and the one on the right to Woolwich, for the
road behind her going upwards, and in front
of her going downwards, was but the same
great one. She used to stop for a moment
quite punctually at a quarter past nine and
look down the one that led to Woolwich,

wondering if by chance the soldiers were coming and with them their band. If there was
no sign of them she would look to the left towards Eltham. At Eltham was an old palace
that had a moat, and on the edge of the moat
a crane stood on one leg. She always lingered
on the bridge leading to the palace to look at
the moat and wonder what the crane thought
about. She felt it had lived for hundreds of
years, and remembered Henry VIII. and Anne
Boleyn dancing in the great hall that was now
a ruin : and she wished she had been alive in
those days to entreat the King not to cut off
Anne's head.

But she never had time to linger at the
cross-roads ; the fear of Uncle Robert was before her eyes, still more of the tale-telling of
Susan Barnes, who had looked after the house
since Aunt Evelina's death. So leaving her
dreams of romance behind she walked on half
a mile and, just as she came in sight of the
mile-stone in the distance, stopped at a long
low white house on the left. The house had a

little narrow garden in front and green Vene·
tian blinds to its windows, that winter and
summer were always open.   This was Mrs.
Barrett's school.   Katherine went as a morning pupil, from half-past nine to one, and carried a mighty list of lessons back with her to
learn in the drawing-room of the White House
by Severndroog.   She hardly knew her school-
fellows, for Mr. Morris (her uncle) did not
wish her to make friends, and allowed no
visitors.   But the school-hours were happy
enough, for Mrs. Barrett was fond of the little
lonely girl, and looked at her in a somewhat
kindlier fashion than she did at the rest of her
pupils;   and once—this was when she was
twelve years old—she gave her as a birthday
gift a little black satin workbag embroid-
ered with forget-me-nots.   Katherine kept it
hidden away in a drawer, and thought it too
precious a thing even to look at very often.

At one o'clock she sallied forth from her
school along the road again, never forgetting
to turn her head when she came to the turn-

ings to the right and left, and went up the hill and back to the White House. Susan Barnes was always waiting with a sharp eye to see whether she had dust or mud on her shoes, and a quick injunction to get ready for dinner. After dinner—she ate it alone four days a week—she worked at her lessons till tea-time : then Uncle Robert came home. ,

"Well, what have you been doing?" he would ask. She answered nothing, for she was always in awe of him. " Behaved yourself, eh ?" On Susan's answer depended the rest of the day.

"Oh, she's been tiresome, as usual," the woman would say sometimes—"started five minutes late for school and no one knows what she did coming back—it was five-and-twenty minutes past one by the clock before she entered the gate, and then, instead of having her gloves on, she carried them all in a screw."

"Oh, that was it ! I suppose you were thinking of the soldiers or watching for the

band : well, that's to make you do it again ! "
and he would give her a cuff on the ears.
Then she hid herself away to cry, but did
not hate him in the least, for she remembered
that just as he scolded her now so he used
to scold her Aunt Evelina.   It was only a matter of course.

If Susan gave a good report he would
sometimes take her for a walk in the evening.
They generally went up the hill ; he and she
and Martyr, the big black dog.   The road as
it ascended had been cut far back in the old
coaching days so as to make it less steep for
the horses.   On either side was the high foot-
way protected by a hand-rail, and behind it
on the left she could see the top windows of
old-fashioned houses standing a little way
back behind tall fences and garden gates.   On
the right there were hedges and thick trees,
bordering the grounds belonging to more im-
portant dwellings.   Katherine used to think
of the stage coaches as she walked silently
beside her uncle, of the highwaymen, and the

legends of Robin Hood and Maid Marian. On the top of the hill there was an old inn called The Bull, and a little way from the door, against a tree under which the coaches used to draw up, some white stone steps by which the travellers mounted to their places. When she had looked at the inn, she turned her head quickly in order to catch sight of a little path on the other side of the way that led through some woods and round by the back of Severndroog tower and over some fields to Eltham. There were many delights in the woods, for they were full of nut-trees, and in the autumn the nuts hung thick and green, and amid the bracken and briar and underwood the blackberries and wild raspberries trailed. Sometimes, if Uncle Robert were in a good humour, Katherine would push her hand into his—it was not till she was ten or twelve years old that she ventured on this little coaxing— and say, "Let's go through the wood." Perhaps he would say curtly, in a manner that made her feel how absolute was his power—

"No; I want to go another way." Then
they trudged on toward Welling and over
Shoulder - of - Mutton Green, and home by
Plumstead Lane—a long walk for a little girl;
it made her feet sore and aching. But there
were compensations, especially in September
when a flock of geese waddled over the
Green; or in June when they went down
Plumstead Lane and past the strawberry-garden. Once or twice in the summer after Mr.
Belcher first came from town and went back
again when he had had some tea and seen the
view from the White House windows, Uncle
Robert, in high good humour, took her into
the strawberry-garden. Then she sat in a little
summer-house and ate the reddest strawberries
that ever ripened in the sun, watching the
while some beehives in a far corner. She was
afraid of the bees; but it was a wonderful
thing to think of the inside of the hives, with
a bee asleep in each little cell. In the middle
of the garden was a scarecrow made of two
sticks put crossways and a coat and an old

hat, with a mask for a face, and each armless sleeve had a strawberry pottle sewn to the end of it. It was worth being footsore and weary to go to the strawberry-garden, or even to pass it by, and to remember that she had seen the geese on the Green and the scarecrow, which was visible enough from the road, and the still beehive, all in one evening.

Or perhaps Uncle Robert would give in about the woods. Then they had a lovely walk : adown the narrow pathway under the trees till they came to the stile—a difficult, awkward stile that Katherine delighted in climbing—through green fields, and over a corn-field in which the poppies grew so thick she could have gathered an armful in two minutes but that she knew Uncle Robert would have strode on without waiting for her, and through the churchyard, against which there were some cottages, as though the dead and the living lived in friendly communion. Thus they went to Eltham, and from Eltham, when they had seen the palace and the crane, they walked along the road Katherine passed on her way to school and so up the hill again to the White House.

But these walks were only in the summer. In the winter-time her daily exercise was confined to going to and fro from Mrs. Barrett's, and sometimes in the afternoon to the post-office and back with Martyr; or, but still less often, to Woolwich with Susan Barnes to shop. When they went to Woolwich they did not go down between the stuffed-bird shop and Ordnance Terrace ; there was a short cut higher up, a little steep way called Constitution Hill, that led into The Lane lower down than where it started from the main road. It came out opposite a public-house called The Eagle, that also had tea-gardens belonging to it. A man with a fair beard was generally standing at the door. He was called Harding, and as she went by he used to say "—Morning, Miss, is the master quite well?" She always answered "Yes, thank you, Mr. Harding," and walked on demurely beside Susan Barnes, who never condescended even to look at him : for though Susan seldom went to church she had very strong opinions, and considered that Mr. Harding was a publican and a sinner. The walk to Woolwich was an event in her quiet life—under the trees on the common and on through the white gate towards the Artillery barracks, with the wide field in front, and the Rotunda in the distance : sometimes the band was playing, or the soldiers being drilled on the parade as she and Susan went down towards the narrow streets of the town. If Susan's manner relaxed in the bustle of shopping, she would take Katherine into the confectioner's at Green's End, and say in her hard, respectful voice :

" Better sit down and eat a cheese-cake or two, Miss Katherine ; it's a long way back."

Katherine used to wonder, as they went up the hill in the cold, grey twilight of the winter, why so many people came to live in the world, and what they all thought about it, and whether they felt as she did, that it was

full of mysteries and barriers. But after all
if life was occasionally a dull thing to her
and some days had their blows or bitternesses,
there was the expectancy of youth in her
heart, and the waiting for the unknown that
makes all things seem like passing clouds.
The winter evenings were difficult to get
through. She sat in the drawing-room alone,
and was supposed to sew till eight o'clock;
but she used to get up now and then to play
at battledore and shuttlecock: for the drawing-room was not crowded with furniture like
those of modern days, and there was a wide
space between the round table and the grand
piano. At eight o'clock she went down-stairs
to say good-night to Uncle Robert, and stayed
in the dining-room to drink a glass of milk
and eat three picnic biscuits before going
to bed.

This was her life till she was nearly fourteen. Then one morning just as Uncle Robert
was getting ready to go to town a letter came
with many foreign stamps upon it: when he

had read it he turned to Katherine with a face so drawn and strange that she was frightened.

"Go and fetch Susan," he said. Susan went into the dining-room and shut the door. Katherine did not dare enter in upon them, besides it was time to get ready for school ; but when she came downstairs five minutes later, she could hear that Susan was sobbing, and her heart warmed to the stern old woman who had taken care of her since she was a little girl. She opened the dining-room door a little way and said softly, "May I come in?" And Susan answered in a kinder voice than usual, "Yes, come along, Miss, and you must not go to school to-day."

So Katherine went up and put her arms round Susan and looked at Uncle Robert, who stood quite still and almost rigid by the table, on which the open letter was lying.

"Mr. Richard is dead," Susan said. "I knew him since he was a baby."

"When did he die?" Katherine whispered, awestruck.

2

"We don't know," Susan answered, wiping away her tears, "but you must have a black frock before you can be seen about again. You won't go to town, Sir, to-day, I suppose?" she asked Mr. Morris.

"Yes, I shall go; I want to see Belcher." And slowly buttoning his coat, Mr. Morris went out and down the pathway to the garden gate with slow hesitating steps, as though he had been half-stunned.

"Ah," said Susan, as she looked after him shaking her head. "He's had a blow from which he'll find it hard to rise. He thought he knew the worst, but he was mistaken."

"Who was Mr. Richard?" Katherine asked.

"He was your Uncle Robert's only son."

"And where has he been?"

There was some hesitation in Susan's manner before she answered—

"He has been in Australia, and other parts. He went away," she added with still more hesitation, "before you were born. He never thought to see him again, but he never thought to hear that he was dead; it was bad enough without that. Well, it killed his mother years ago."

"What killed her?"

"Mr. Richard. He did what was wrong and had to go away—they sent him away," she added in a low voice. "They knew he'd never come back, but they thought perhaps some day he'd be all right out there. He is no relation of yours, really," Susan Barnes added. "You belong to the mistress's side of the family; so you needn't think there's anything bad in your blood—not that there was in his either. What he did he was led to do."

"Susan," Katherine asked, "have I any relations besides Uncle Robert? I didn't know there was Mr. Richard."

"Not a soul that I know of. You were the daughter of the mistress's sister—half-sister she was, and years and years younger—and there were no more of them, but just those two. Mistress married master, and your moth-

er married a clergyman, who died and left her
with nothing. It was lucky for you that your
Aunt Evelina took you. But for her, you
hadn't a relation in the world nor a stock or
stone belonging to you."

Then Katherine asked a question that had
often puzzled her.

"Did Uncle Robert like Aunt Evelina?"

"Oh, yes, he liked her well enough; but
he was always a hard man, and had his way
wherever he went, and sometimes she'd sit
down and cry about it instead of getting up
and doing what he wanted. If he'd been a bit
softer with Mr. Richard, things wouldn't have
been so hard for himself now."

"Are they hard for him?" she asked wonderingly.

"Yes, and they have been, and if they
hadn't it would have been different for you.
He wouldn't have cuffed you so often—I believe he's fond of you in his way; but men are
always hard on women; they've got the upper
hand, and they know it—and the only thing

we can do is to make the best of it. After all, they earn the money, and they've the right to be master." Then Susan went to the window and pulled down the blind.

"What is that for?" Katherine asked, for she knew nothing about death.

"It's for Mr. Richard—I wouldn't like to think we didn't make the house dark a single day for him. It may be months since he died, but it's only this morning we heard of it. You are all your Uncle Robert's got left in the world now, Miss Katherine. There's Mr. Belcher, he thinks a lot of him, and——"

The rest of Susan's speech was lost as she went upstairs to pull down the bed-room blinds. Katherine felt as if she had looked out a little farther into the world, and had drawn back disheartened, for she had only learnt that Mr. Richard had gone wrong and died, and that Aunt Evelina had broken her heart.

Since she was not to go to school that day, she sat still for a while and thought about all manner of things that did not directly concern herself. For as yet she had not realised that she was anything more than a creature allowed almost as a favour to live in the world and look on at the people and the things that were in it. That she had an individuality of her own, and a life to live, a capacity to suffer and rejoice—that she was, in fact, heiress in common with the rest of her sex to all the possibilities of humanity—had not yet dawned upon her. She was only a lonely school girl, whom experience had taught to submit, and whose sense concerning the future was just the curious one of waiting.

Susan's revelations, such as they were, drew her nearer to Uncle Robert. She had always wanted to like him, but had been half afraid. Now she knew that any harshness he had shown her had not been unkindness so much as an expression of many things he had suffered himself : she felt a little frightened tenderness towards him, and wondered if she could do anything that would please him. She remembered that there

were some wall-flowers growing in the garden,
at the far end behind the bank of laurel : she
was certain he did not know they were there.
She had stood over them every morning before
he was down, and softly touched their petals :
they felt like velvet, and she liked, too, the
little close bunches of dark buds. Perhaps he
would be pleased if she gathered some into one
of the blue and white bowls, and put it on the
square table in the middle of his bedroom.
Once or twice her pupils had taken Mrs.
Barrett a bouquet of flowers to school ; one of
them gave her a little brass bowl on her birthday filled with violets, and Mrs. Barrett had
put it on the drawing-room table, and looked
happy all day because of it. Perhaps Uncle
Robert would be pleased too. So in the afternoon she took down the bowl and went to the
garden without Susan seeing her, for she did
not want anyone to know what she was going
to do : she felt as if it would take away from
its tenderness. She filled the bowl with water
from the pump that was just outside the house,

so full that it brimmed over, and went along
the pathway under the beech and larch trees,
and disappeared behind the laurel bank and
put it down beside her while she gathered the
flowers, carefully sorting the shades of brown.
Then she rose up from her knees, and was
about to carry it in her two hands back to the
house. As she passed the back door, painted
grey and with a little heap of stones beside it,
that led out on to the main road, a key turned
in the lock. Mr. Morris and a tall dark man
of about two-and-thirty entered the garden so
quickly that Katherine started and dropped
the bowl, which scattered itself with the water
and flowers at her feet.

"What does this mean?" Mr. Morris asked.
"What are you doing?" She looked up at him
with a white face and two blue eyes full of fright.

"I was going to put some flowers in your
room—because you were unhappy," she said in
a low voice.

The tall man with Uncle Robert almost
laughed ; she saw it and turned away.

"I thought you would be pleased," she went on in a still lower voice, as if she resented being heard by any one else.

Mr. Morris looked at her for a moment in silence.

"Well, never mind," he said in a hard voice, "have that mess swept up: you oughtn't to pick flowers without asking leave. I don't want to see you again to-day." He walked towards the house without another word, and Mr. Belcher, as the other man was called, followed him. She stooped and gathered up the flowers in one hand and ruefully put the bits of broken bowl into a heap, and standing on the heap of stones, threw them over the garden fence into the ditch behind. Every morning for a week afterwards she used to see them on her way to school, till, unable to bear the sight any longer, she surreptitiously buried them.

Then she hid herself behind the laurels, and putting her gathered flowers a little way from her, gave way to bitter disappointment, till hiding her face in her arms on the little

grassy bank, she broke down altogether, and
sobbed. Presently she heard the sound of a
footstep and started. Mr. Belcher was coming
towards her with the amused expression still
on his face.

"In disgrace, eh?" he asked, insultingly it
seemed to Katherine. She rose to her feet and
stood looking at him, while a strange dismay
took possession of her. He was a tall man
and dark, not thin, and with something determined in his gait. He had brown eyes, cold
and large, and dark hair that had been carefully brushed and parted on one side; it was
not thick, and it lay very close to his head.
He had a rather long upper lip, closely shaven,
a firmly shut mouth, and little side whiskers.
Though he was only two-and-thirty he looked
older, and like one a good deal taken up with
the affairs of life: keen, and with an eye to
main chances. There was something method-
ical in his manner and almost cruel in his expression: Katherine quailed a little before it,
but did not know that she was afraid of him.

"I thought he would be pleased," she said sullenly.

"People are seldom pleased when you break their crockery: you should be more careful." She did not answer a word. He measured her with his eyes. "Why, you are growing quite tall, Katherine, how old are you—fifteen?"

"I am fourteen." He looked at her again.

"Come and walk round the garden," he said. She hesitated and did not move. "Come," he repeated with a little masterful smile, "a walk will do you good."

Reluctantly she went forward step by step, and walked beside him round the big untidy garden, under the beech and larch trees, beside the marigold-bed which did not yet show a sign of life, and towards the little clump of primroses that only she knew to be breaking into bloom. She would not even look towards it while she was with Mr. Belcher, she felt it would be cruel to betray them to him: and luckily he did not see them.

"I should make something of this garden if the place were mine," he said almost to himself.

"Uncle Robert likes it as it is," Katherine answered in a low voice, her soul full of opposition to everything he said. They walked on again for a minute or two in silence, he still looking at her now and again with a curious smile.

"Shall I ask your uncle to forgive you for breaking the bowl?" he asked mockingly.

"It doesn't matter," she answered, the tears coming into her eyes again.

"If I were you I'd take care not to offend him; he has a good bit of money to leave behind, and if you play your cards well it may come to you now." He said it with a meaning look and a nod of his head that for some unknown reason made her hate him.

CHAPTER II.

DURING the next three years, those that followed on the news of Richard Morris's death, Katherine felt herself to be under the dominion not only of her Uncle Robert but of Mr. Belcher. Mr. Morris appeared to grow fonder of her, but he silently controlled every action of her life—so that she did not dare to spend a single hour in a manner of which he would have disapproved. The sense of his authority directed even the lonely walks in the Eltham Woods which Susan Barnes sometimes allowed her to take on summer afternoons. She never dared to stay among the nut-trees and blackberry bushes to day-dream or wonder about the future, but walked on methodically and sedately, so that she might

not fail to get into the time she was out the
right amount of exercise. Her school lessons
went on regularly, though Mrs. Barrett's
pupils decreased in number, for the school-
mistress meant to retire in a year or two, and
had lost her eagerness. When she was six-
teen, Katherine made friends with Alice
Irvine, the daughter of an officer quartered at
Woolwich, a pretty girl, who went to Mrs.
Barrett's chiefly to fill out her time, for she
was nineteen and supposed to have finished
her education. The friendship soon came to
an end, for Alice Irvine went to India with
her father and the solitary break in the monotony of Katherine's girlhood ended. Mr.
Belcher appeared regularly every Saturday.
She understood that he always came on business, and was solicitor to some Company of
which her uncle was chief director, and they
evidently had a great deal to talk over. He
seemed to manage Mr. Morris's affairs, and
gained an ascendancy over him till he almost
ruled the house.

On the day she was seventeen a strange thing happened. She had hitherto on her birthday had a cake covered with white sugar. It was severely put on to the tea-table by Susan Barnes, and though Katherine was allowed to cut it, she was not allowed to eat it at will—it had to serve the household for the next fortnight, and always to be undertaken with an air of responsibility. But it was the yearly recognition of her childhood, and Katherine looked forward to it. This time when Susan Barnes asked a week before if she was to make Miss Katherine's cake, Mr. Morris looked at her wonderingly.

"Cake?" he said severely; "why, no, she'll be seventeen. A young woman! What does a young woman want with cake?" Then when Susan had left the room he turned and looked at his niece as if he were considering some momentous question concerning her.

"You are very tall," he said at last, "you have your mother's blue eyes and dark hair. I suppose you're pretty," he added grimly.

"I don't know what I'm going to do with you ; in another year or two you ought to be getting a husband."

It was the queerest thing to say, Katherine thought, as she went to school. It opened a vista of life in a part of the world that was not Shooter's Hill, and with somebody who was not Uncle Robert. When her birthday came it was on a Saturday, and Mrs. Barrett gave her a copy of "Lalla Rookh" in a dark binding with gilt edges and a narrow green ribbon marker.

"We shall separate soon, my dear Katherine," she said tremulously, "but you have been my favourite pupil, and I shall always remember you. I shall retire in another year, but perhaps your uncle will consider that your education is finished even before that period, and wish to take you away."

"I hope not," Katherine answered. "I should be so sorry to leave you." And she thought how dreary it would be to live morning after morning without passing the two roadways she had looked down all her life. Still, she was growing older, and she realised it, even while she stood looking at her school-mistress and the familiar school-desks, and thought curiously of the world beyond the soldiers and band, on the one side, and the moat and immovable crane on the other. There were times when a strange eagerness came over her, so that she felt she could have run along the great Dover Road, over the hill and past the Bull through Welling and Bexley, and on and on till she saw the white cliffs on the far-away coast. She was like a bird flapping its wings before it dared to fly. Some day, she felt, without knowing that she did so, they would bear her far away.

Mr. Belcher had arrived when she returned. She wished Uncle Robert had been alone, and that he and she had been going for one of the old long walks together in the afternoon. "I think he would have been kind to me," she thought.

"Seventeen, I understand, Katherine," Mr.

3

Belcher said. "Seventeen is always considered grown-up for a young lady. I have
brought you a present." He said it in a voice
that sounded like a dominant note in her life,
and he produced a brown leather case, the like
of which she had never seen except in the
shop windows at Woolwich. Her hands
trembled as she pressed the spring and dis-
closed a little gold neck-chain, from which
was suspended a heart covered with tur-
quoises.

"Is this for me?" she asked with a wondering smile. "Oh, thank you, Mr. Belcher.
It is kind of you."

"Mind you take care of it," he answered,
looking at a dimple in her cheek. "I don't
think the snap is very strong."

"I have a present for you too, Katherine,"
Mr. Morris said, knitting his shaggy eyebrows
together. "But I waited till Belcher came before I gave it to you. Here it is, my dear."
Something in his voice made Katherine's heart
bound, while a sob that was half joy rose in

her throat. Then he too gave her a case, and in it was a little gold watch.

"Perhaps it may be useful to you," he added apologetically, as if he were half ashamed of giving her anything ornamental.

"Oh, it is lovely!" she sighed, full of joyful surprise. She borrowed an old guard of Susan's and put it round her neck, and tucked the watch into her waistband, and felt that the day was a happy one.

She wandered about the garden in the afternoon and peered over the fence toward the woods, and wished she could scurry away round by Severndroog and over the fields and through the churchyard to Eltham. Then she looked round and saw Mr. Belcher.

"We are to go for a walk," he said.

"Is Uncle Robert coming too?"

"No," he answered shortly, "we are going alone. Come, I saw your hat in the hall."

She followed him meekly into the house, not daring to refuse. He reached down her hat and her little tweed cloak that hung be-

neath it; there were some gloves in the
pocket; and she walked out beside him, down
the pathway and through the gate, and on
to the main road. He hesitated a moment.
"We'll go over the hill," he said, and she
gave a sigh of relief; for she had been so
afraid he would go to the woods. They
walked on in silence for ten minutes. Every
now and then he looked at her in a curious,
half-doubtful manner. When he spoke it almost made her start.

"Well, what do you think of being seventeen?" he asked.

She thought of the new experiences the
day had brought and answered with a little
sigh, "I think it is very nice."

"What do you suppose will happen to you
in the future?"

"I cannot tell," she said, looking forward
at the long white road that stretched into
the distance. Then, just as they were passing The Bull, he asked a surprising question—

"Do you think you would like to go and live in London?"

"I don't know," she answered doubtfully. "There are so many people, and there are no——" She was going to say woods, but she would not remind him of them lest he should want to turn down the narrow pathway on the right that led to one she knew. "—there are no walks."

"You could drive in the park or go to the theatre. Perhaps some day, if you get a good husband—— do you think you'd like a husband, Katherine?"

"No," she answered shortly. "I am not old enough yet."

His steps slackened for a moment; he looked at the road ahead and hesitated.

"We won't go any farther this way," he said decisively, and turned round quickly. They retraced their steps till they passed the Bull again. Just a few yards below it, turning off on the right, was a road overhung by trees. It looked still and deserted.

"Where does this lead to?" he asked.

"It is Shrewsbury Lane; it leads to Plum Lane. But it is getting late, and——"

"Plenty of time," he answered; "come along," and Katherine helplessly followed. She pulled out her watch and turned it over and looked at it, thinking she was unobserved.

"You'd better take care of that watch," he said; "he gave a good deal for it. I was with him when he bought it."

"I wasn't thinking of that," she said; "I was thinking that it was very kind of him to give it me—it was very kind of you to give me the chain, Mr. Belcher."

"Do you like ornaments?"

She considered for a moment.

"Yes, I think so," she said—and they went on a little way in silence. Then she spoke again. "If we lived in London we should get a great many more books; but I should be afraid to go about alone, and there would be no places to sketch—I had some lessons at

Mrs. Barrett's," she added hurriedly, "and the country is so lovely."

"You could walk about alone if you were married," he said, and looked at her meaningly ; but she answered nothing.

They came to a narrow pathway that turned off on to the left and led downwards through an undergrowth of brake and briar to Woolwich Common.

"This looks like a quiet way," he said ; "we'll try it."

"It's longer round.   We should be late for Uncle Robert."

"Plenty of time," he said again decisively : and again she followed him.   It was a lonely path, there was not a soul within sight or sound.   She lingered a little way behind ; but he stopped and waited for her.   "Take my arm," he said.   She shrank back in visible dismay, but he held it out, and she did as he told her.   "You'll never get married if you behave like that," he said, "a wife always takes her husband's arm and walks beside him."

She did not answer a word, but a little fright crept into her heart and stayed there all that day and put a mark on the months that followed.

At the end of the year she left school. Mrs. Barrett's health failed, and she went away to live with a sister in the country: so the windows of the house down the road were closed, and a padlock put on the gate.

This was at the beginning of the winter. Katherine was growing older and impatient; her uncle was rather kinder to her, perhaps, but he held aloof as much as ever. She had sketched nearly every point in the neighbourhood, and read all the books in the house, carrying them usually to the steps of Severndroog Tower. She found it better to sit there in the sunshine safely hidden from everything, save the crows and the trees, than to go to the woods with their bare twigs and soddened pathways and the frightened rabbits that scuttled through the underwood. Mr. Belcher came as much as ever, and his manner towards her was different. He did not talk to her much, but he looked at her a good deal, and there was something in his expression that made her fear him and invent excuses for hurrying out of sight as much as possible on the Saturdays he spent at the White House.

Then a change came.

Susan Barnes fell ill and kept her bed for weeks, while Katherine nursed her, and gained, at the same time, some knowledge of housekeeping. After a time Susan grew better, but she would never be good for anything again, the doctor said ; and she pleaded to be allowed to go to her own people at Bridgewater to end her days. Then, as if to complicate matters further, the owner of the White House refused to renew Mr. Morris's lease, and Katherine knew that he was discussing closely with Mr. Belcher the question of where to live if he had to seek another home. He was growing old ; the news of his son's death had put twenty years on to him ; the journeys to and fro from London tried him sorely, his silences were longer,

his instincts seemed to develop more and more
strongly in the direction of solitude. Even on
his walks he no longer asked her to accompany
him, and, stern and silent, turned away from
her half-appealing look as he left the house
and went on his way alone. She tried singing
to him once; music-lessons had been included
in her course at Mrs. Barrett's, and the old-
fashioned school-mistress had taken care that
she learnt old English songs, and the new-
fashioned teacher had seen that the German
ones were not left out. She had the fresh
young voice of a thrush, but he only looked
at her coldly for a moment and said, "Keep
your songs for when I am out of doors; I don't
care for music."

"He is a hard man," Susan muttered, "and
no one could ever get round him—though Mr.
Belcher seems pretty nigh doing it."

"Susan," asked Katherine, "must you go
away? I will do all your work for you, and
take such care of you if you will stay, you
dear old Susan;" and she put her arms round

the old woman's neck ; but Susan did not respond very kindly. During the long years spent in his service she had learnt something of her master's coldness and reserve.

"I am going to my own people, Miss Katherine," she said, "I don't want to spend all my days in service."

"But you have been all my days with me," the girl answered, "don't you like me ?" She only said "like" and felt a little shy even of that.

"Oh, yes, Miss Katherine ; I like you, especially since you've grown older ; you were very tiresome about not taking care of your things when you were young. But I want to go to my home—one's own is one's own all the world over."

The one little pleasure of those months, oddly enough, came through Mr. Belcher. It was in the shape of a bull pup. He brought it down with him for the first time one day late in October, a white and black pugnacious thing, with a queer ugly face and a brisk tail,

and a loose, wrinkled skin that had a very
little body inside it. It was called "Dottel,"
and took to Katherine immediately, and con-
soled her for Martyr's absolute indifference,
for the old black retriever cared for no one
but his master, and nothing but the door-mat
on which he lay from morning to night. She
found herself watching once or twice for Mr.
Belcher's coming, simply because it meant that
she would see Dottel pattering beside him,
slow and heavy, but ready to snarl and snap
on the least provocation. She used to beguile
him down the garden and through the back
gate by which she had once broken the flower-
bowl, on to the main road, and across to the
post-office, where they sold chocolates, and
back again, round the corner by the wall,
and along the Severndroog road and through
a gate into a brambly untidy field, and disappear with him through the trees at the end
till she came to the tower and the little open
space around it. Then she would sit down
with Dottel on the steps and talk to him,

and pull up his skin in ruts upon his body, and tell him that he was hideous—"a dear dog, but very hideous."

Thus came an end to many things. Quite suddenly one afternoon in midwinter, as the twilight was coming on, Mr. Belcher appeared, just as he had appeared before her long ago behind the laurel bank.

"Oh, that's it, is it?" he said, with his odd smile. "I wondered where it was you hid yourself so often. It's getting late; come back." He gave Dottel a little kick: the dog growled and showed his teeth for answer.

"I don't want to go back just yet," she said.

"It's time," he answered curtly. "Come, I've something to say to you."

With the habit of obedience to his sex strong upon her, she rose and stood before him as if waiting for his next command.

"Take my arm," he said, "it's getting dark." They went back under the trees, over the brambly field, and towards the gate; but,

instead of opening it, he stopped and leant on
it, and looked at her triumphantly. The twilight was gathering closer and closer round
them, but he could see her face plainly—a
girl's face with grey-blue eyes and a mass of
dark hair coiled tightly round her head.
" She'll be a good-looking woman some day,"
he thought. "I believe she's as tall as I am
now," and he mentally measured her height.

"Let me see," he said, "how old are you,
Katherine?"

" Eighteen."

"Time for that husband we talked about."

"Please don't say that," she answered, and
her hand sought the latch of the gate. He
firmly lifted it off.

"That is what I mean to talk about," he
answered. "You can't go on living here for
ever. Do you think you would like to be married?"

"I never think about it, I am not old
enough."

"Eighteen's quite old enough. A man

doesn't want to marry a frump." He put his face nearer to hers. "Give me a kiss," he said.

"Oh, don't!" she exclaimed, with a little cry that was half terror and half surprise. "Please let me go back." She stooped towards Dottel, who was wandering round her feet and trying one uncomfortable attitude after another.

"Nonsense!" he said, with another laugh, as if her resistance were part of a game. "Don't you think you'd like to marry me?" She looked up as if she thought he had gone mad.

"Marry you, Mr. Belcher? Oh, no! Why, you are too old." It was said in sheer bewilderment, and without any offence in her voice.

"Thirty-six," he answered; "excellent difference—the man should be a good bit older."

Thirty-six seemed a long way on towards middle age to Katherine, who remembered him a grown man ever since she was a little girl. Moreover, Mr. Belcher, though he was moder-

ately tall, was a little inclined to stoutness of
figure, which added to his years, and his trim
whiskers and manner of dressing did not take
away from them. Katherine was silent for a
moment. Then she pleaded—

"Do let me go home, Mr. Belcher. Uncle
Robert will be expecting us."

"He knows all about it. Highly approves ;
and said we'd better settle it up at once. Do
you think you'll like living in London?"

"Uncle Robert knows and approves?" she
said, unbelievingly.

"Yes, of course he does. So you'd better
give me that kiss."

She shrank back with dread. An expression shot from his eyes that showed that he
would reckon with her by and by.

"Oh ! very well," he said, with a disagreeable laugh, "if you'd rather not. You will
have to come to it, and you'll find it much
more amusing to take me the right way than
to take me the wrong one. Come, we'll go
back : then you can ask your uncle. I should

think you must know by this time that when
he has made up his mind to a thing he'll carry
it through." He closed the gate after them as
they went on to the Severndroog road. "Perhaps it's as well to tell you at once that it's my
method also, so come along"; and with a jerk
he pulled her hand through his arm. "I shall
take you to the theatre, and give you some
pleasure now and then if you are a good
girl," he added as he drew her reluctantly
along. It was not five minutes to the house.
As they reached the garden he pulled up and
looked at her with an air of proprietorship;
while Dottel, waddling on in front, stopped
as if he, too, had something to do with the
matter.

"Where is Uncle Robert?" she asked
scornfully.

"Waiting for you—he wants to give us his
blessing. Why, Katherine, you'll be Mrs. Edward Belcher, and live in Montague Place, and
look after the house and sit at the head of the
table. Rather different from Shooter's Hill
4

and going to school ? You ought to be quite
pleased."

She did not speak a word till they reached
the house. Then she turned and faced him.

"I want to see Uncle Robert alone," she
said haughtily. And, leaving him in doubt
whether to follow her or not, she entered the
dining-room and shut the door. Mr. Morris
was sitting over the fire.

"Uncle Robert," she asked in dismay, the
excitement she had suppressed in the inter-
view that had just taken place flashing from
her eyes, and indignant incredulity making itself heard in her voice, "you don't want me to
marry Mr. Belcher, do you ? "

Mr. Morris looked up at her for a moment
in silence.

"Yes, I do," he answered firmly. "He
will make you a good husband and I shall
know that you are taken care of. He is well
off, and——"

"Oh, but I can't, indeed ! " she cried, clasping her hands. "It would be dreadful."

"That is only because you are young, my dear," he answered kindly, but with determination that sounded like a decree, "and don't know what is best for you. I have thought it well over, and the thing is settled. Belcher will be very kind to you——"

"But why can't I stay with you? I don't want to go away."

"I am going away. I must, for the lease of this house is up. I am very lonely since my son died," he added in a lower voice. "Probably I shall take rooms in London near a club."

"Let me stay with you there," she pleaded, and put her hand on his. But he shook his head.

"I want to be alone," he answered, "and I am getting old, Katherine, and want to see you settled. I have done the best I can for you, and have told Belcher what my intentions are, so that he'll have every reason to be good to you. Now go away, my dear, and don't be foolish."

"I can't be married to him, uncle. I don't like him."

"You'll like him by and by, if he's good to you."

"Let me stay with Susan——"

"Nonsense! I tell you the thing is settled, we know what is best for you. Now go away," and he took up his newspaper again. She went out of the room, nearly falling over Martyr, who whined and moved out of her way.

"I must put a brick-bat round that poor old brute's neck and give him a wet bath," she heard her uncle say, "he's only a misery to himself and everyone else."

It was like a Fate-day Katherine thought, and she remembered a mystical story she had read the year before in which lives to live were dealt out to the people and there was no escape for them.

Dottel was on the stairs; he got up uneasily as she passed, went up a step or two after her, then, as if he had changed his mind, stopped and waddled down again, and went out to seek his master, who stood by the garden-door, waiting in calm certainty till Katherine had given over her foolish struggles and recognised the inevitable.

"Susan," Katherine said, creeping up to the woman, who was lying in the dark on her bed, "are you better? Can I talk to you?".

" Yes, come and sit down side of me, here, Miss Katherine. I'm better." Susan raised her pillows and turned her head round till Katherine could see the clear unflinching eyes looking at her through the shadow.

"Susan," she exclaimed, as if she felt that her news would bewilder her listener, "they want me to marry Mr. Belcher; *me*—me, to marry——"

"Well, Miss," and Susan raised her head a little higher. The girl sat down on the bed despairingly, for those two words betrayed that Susan too would be against her: so that, breaking down, she pleaded her own cause badly.

"But, Susan, he is so much older—and I am so young—and I don't want to be married, and I don't like him."

"If he makes you a good husband, you'll like him after a bit." Oh, those terrible words, "a good husband!" There was something hopeless in the sound of them.

"But I can't, Susan." And she burst into tears and put her face down on the bedclothes that covered the woman's chest. "I don't want to be married. I don't want anything different, and I can't bear him," she sobbed. "Uncle Robert says I must, and Mr. Belcher——"

Susan raised herself still a little more and tried to hold her.

"Look here, Miss Katherine," she said, "your uncle knows what's best, and he's made up his mind, and you'll have to do it. Men's master, and we've got to give way to them. You'll find that out all through life, and you must just make the best of it. If he gives you a good home and is kind to you, you'll get on all right. Just don't make a fuss about it," she said kindly, drawing her arm tighter round the slim shoulders.

"But I hate Mr. Belcher," Katherine whispered with a shudder.

"And I don't like him," Susan said, as if the words were dragged from her. "Never did. I expect he's a hard man; but," she went on doggedly, "men are hard—that's what women have to find out, and the wisest just says nothing and makes the best of them. You take my advice, Miss Katherine, and submit. You'll feel better when you're settled down in a home of your own."

"I like this home."

"This isn't going to be one for any of us much longer. The lease is up, the master's getting older, and I believe he wants to make a change in his life; and me—I'm going home to Bridgwater, and they're going to put Martyr into the river before we go. It's all set out by fate"—Katherine raised her head with a jerk, remembering the story-book—" and you'll have to submit."

In six weeks' time she was married to Mr. Belcher.

CHAPTER III.

KATHERINE was too much of a girl to be a companion to her husband, too unsophisticated and inexperienced to hold a man who was not even in love with her. He had nothing to say to her nor she to him. Even their honeymoon, though for the first few days he watched her with a half-curious amusement, bored him : before ten days were over he had discovered a secret amusement in making her wince under those little gibes that he knew would sooner or later have a brutal development. They went to Windermere and stayed at the hotel near the station. The snow still clung high and white to the mountains, but the trees were sprinkled with early green, and the spring flowers were hiding among the tangle of the woods and hedges. The beauty of the scenery took Katherine altogether by surprise. When it first burst upon her in the railway-carriage between Oxenholm and Windermere, the day after her marriage, she gave a cry of joy and bewilderment.

"Oh, it is lovely, it is wonderful!" she said. Her manner pleased Mr. Belcher; he was almost tender as they stood an hour or two later, by the lake's side, and waited for more remarks akin to that one in the train. But Katherine was not in the habit of talking much, and, moreover, had never been on an easy footing with Mr. Belcher, nor, indeed, with anyone in her whole life except, perhaps, her school friend Alice Irvine. She looked up at the great hills and felt the beauty of the whole place wrap round and round her like a dream of which she was in the midst; but, like a dreamer, she had no words to say to the living man beside her. They took long walks almost in silence, while he thought of matters wholly unconnected with his surroundings,

and she felt the world stretch itself out before
her eyes and realised how little she knew concerning it. Sometimes during that first week
Mr. Belcher used to look at her half con-
temptuously as she sat back in the boat which
the sturdy North-countrymen rowed across
the lake, or along the edge beneath the
shadow of the mountains, and wonder how he
was to get through the next three weeks
allowed to his honeymoon, with a schoolgirl
in a serge frock and a sailor hat. It bored him
after a time even to worry her.

Then, luckily, they made acquaintance
with a Mr. and Mrs. Oswell, who were staying
at the hotel. He was a barrister of forty, dark
and slim and leisurely, with kind grey eyes
that gave Katherine a sense of safety when she
looked at them. In some undefined manner it
floated through her mind that if Mr. Belcher
were cruel, Mr. Oswell would protect her. He
seemed to be fond of his wife. Katherine
used to see them walking up and down together in front of the hotel, after dinner, evi-

dently engrossed in each other's conversation. Sometimes she heard them laughing as if they were amused ; or if they were silent it was the silence of two people who were companions. "I can feel that they are married," Katherine thought. "They are like the husband and wife one reads about : they are very different from us." She could not imagine that a time would ever come when she and Mr. Belcher would walk up and down and talk in a low voice, and be content together.

At first sight Mrs. Oswell was hardly equal to her husband ; she was a tall, handsome woman, with a good many rings on her fingers, and clothes too smart for a country hotel. She was about two or three and thirty, perhaps ; and had a manner that was a little masterful, but it gave way immediately before her husband's quiet one. She took pains to be agreeable to Mr. Belcher, chiefly because her husband had taken a violent dislike to him, "which is thoroughly immoral of you, Fred," she remarked. "Mr. Belcher is a solicitor, and rich ; I can see it in the cut of his frock-coat at the table-d'hôte, and you are the inevitable barrister. The rest need not be explained."

" I hate the look of him, and I am certain that he bullies that unlucky girl he has married. I saw a horrible smile on his face yesterday, when he had evidently said something that made her miserable."

" Probably there's something to be said on both sides," Mrs. Oswell answered. " He can be polite if it is expected of him : she expects him to behave like a tyrant, so he does."

The Oswells and the Belchers had a little square table to themselves that night. Mrs. Oswell, perhaps on purpose, informed Mr. Belcher in the intimate manner of people who have been together three days on board ship or a week in the same hotel, how many presents her husband made her, and how terribly she bullied him, though she humoured him sometimes.

" Do you make your wife many presents,

Mr. Belcher？" she asked. "You look like a generous man."

"I should make a wife like you a great many," he answered, with a smile that was meant to be fascinating.

"Perhaps she does not humour you enough. Mrs. Belcher," she went on, "always humour men ; it never does to be too strict with them." Katherine, who felt that Mrs. Oswell was a good-natured but rather vulgar person, merely smiled across her soup.

"I don't think I shall find my wife too strict," Mr. Belcher said significantly.

"Beast !" thought Mr. Oswell. "I'll bet that girl runs away from him or breaks her heart before she is five years older." Then there followed a conversation that Katherine was to remember all her life, for every word seemed to burn itself upon her brain as though it were a portion of her history ; and yet the subject seemed a trivial one. "When you have been married as long as I have," Mr. Oswell said to Mr. Belcher, trying to make things easier for her, "you won't be so confident. Still, I manage to get my own way sometimes—eh, Bee? Do you remember when you had set your heart on going to Ventnor, and I had set mine on a sea voyage?"

"You were a brute," she laughed. "He was indeed, Mrs. Belcher. There are some horrid boats that go to the Mediterranean every week. Will you believe that he beguiled me to Southampton under the impression that I was going to the Isle of Wight, and calmly took me on board one of them, and I sat quite still and innocent, to discover presently that we were on our way to Gibraltar?"

"Excellent experience for you, I should think," Mr. Belcher said, trying to be pleasantly sarcastic.

"You ought to take your wife that trip some day," Mr. Oswell went on; "they are capital boats, picturesque route, and not at all expensive."

"And they go to the Mediterranean?"

asked Katherine. It sounded like the other side of the world.

" They go round by Gibraltar," Mr. Oswell answered, glad to talk to her. "And there you get your first experience of the South. The scent of the orange-trees almost choked me ; and the pepper-trees—long, drooping pink bloom they have—were simply wonderful."

"And such handsome men," Mrs. Oswell put in.

"Yes, go on," Katherine said, not even hearing her. "I would give anything to go abroad."

"Then make your husband take you ; don't give him any peace till he does," Mr. Oswell continued. "It's really an excellent thing to do," he added, turning again to Mr. Belcher. "From Gibraltar—you only stay there a few hours—you get on to Genoa——"

"To Genoa," Katherine repeated longingly.

—"Skirting the shore—seeing Spain and Marseilles as you go by, superb olive-woods

and orange-trees and palms—mountains in the
background, vastly different from these hills,
I can tell you. It is a wonderful thing to go
to Italy for the first time. I like the small
places best myself—little places not overdone
with English people. There are a few of them
along the coast still."

"He ought to live in a tomb," Mrs. Oswell said, laughing; "he delights in being
buried. Naples and Genoa were all very well,
and we picked up all sorts of pretty things at
the shops, but I couldn't bear those dull little
places where the people lived on macaroni
and looked at the sea and the mountains
all day, or went to Mass in the morning, and
spent their evenings around dim little lamps
that didn't even attract the mosquitoes. I
don't care for 'dear, dear abroad'; do you,
Mr. Belcher?"

"I generally stick to England," he answered.

"That's what I like," said Mrs. Oswell;
"give me Scarborough, or even Brighton, and

5

a good spin along the King's Road behind a
pair of horses. What do you say, Mrs.
Belcher?"

But Katherine was feeding Dottel, who had
accompanied them on their honeymoon, and
made no answer. Perhaps Dottel was the only
compensating element in her marriage. He
was growing bigger though not gentler, and
the developing savageness of his nature was
a grim enjoyment to his master, who liked to
see people shrink away from him and draw up
their toes under them.

"Edward," she asked her husband timidly
as they stood by the door together for a few
minutes while the Oswells took their nightly
walk up and down, "do you like Mrs. Oswell?"

"Yes," he said with the leisurely air of
repletion that always beset him after a meal,
"she is the sort of woman I do like."

"She is very good-natured," Katherine said
gently, ashamed of not liking her better;
"but I think she is rather vulgar."

"Oh, nonsense! she has plenty of go. Men like lively women with lots to say for themselves."

Mr. Oswell came up the steps.

"Would you care for a game of billiards?" he asked, while his wife put out her hand towards Katherine.

"Come for a little stroll," she said, "and let our husbands pursue their wicked ways together."

Katherine descended the steps gratefully: a *tête-à-tête* with one of her own sex was virtually a new experience. Mrs. Oswell took her arm and looked at the pale, anxious face; she could see its eager, almost sad, expression even in the twilight; and her heart went out to the slim girl. "It's an excellent thing to shunt our men sometimes. They like us better when they return," she said, trying to be lively. "Don't you think so?"

"I haven't had much experience of shunting them yet," Katherine answered with a laugh, that was almost joyous. Mrs. Oswell,

even though she were vulgar, made her feel
light-hearted, and her manner was distinctly
kindly ; besides, it was a relief to be free
of Mr. Belcher, even for a quarter of an
hour.

"Tell me, how long have you been Madame ?" Mrs. Oswell asked confidentially.
"You look as if it had been the day before
yesterday."

"It was nearly a fortnight ago."

"And was he a widower ?"

"Oh, no ! Why ?"

"He looks it. I am glad he wasn't, can't
torment you with the virtues of his dear de-
parted—probably he'll find some other way,"
she thought. "Why did you marry him ?
Were you very much in love ?"

"I married him," Katherine answered reluctantly, "because my Uncle Robert wished
it, I think. I didn't want to be married so
soon."

"Never mind, it's a good thing over.
There's too much difference in your ages, of

course, but he'll be all right if you manage
him properly. Don't let him bully you."

" Oh, no," Katherine said, rather distantly,
for she did not want to discuss her marriage
with a stranger.

"I always feel so much for men," Mrs. Oswell went on, "we know so little about them.
I feel convinced that you know very little of
Mr. Belcher. A man of his age may have had
all sorts of troubles."

" Trouble ? "

" Oh, yes, you don't know how badly he
was jilted when he was twenty-four, or that he
didn't lose a lot of money later on—or that he
hasn't been bothered to death by relations, or
suffered horrible physical pain and said nothing about it. It never seems to occur to wom-
en how much history a man may have on the
quiet. A woman's career is generally known
to all her intimate friends, and handed on to
her acquaintance ; a man's, as a rule, is only
known to himself—and perhaps to one woman
who doesn't appear."

"I wonder if he has suffered things——"
Katherine said, looking out towards the lake,
and feeling, as she did so, that Mrs. Oswell
was pushing open the gate of life a little
wider.

"Disagreeable people generally have ; and
you know, my dear, he does look disagreeable
sometimes. I say it to reconcile you to it. I
always feel as if they were distributing round
the knocks they have received themselves.
But don't let him bully you. He's the sort
of man who will if he can. Look very good-
tempered, and laugh at him when he begins."

"You always seem to be laughing, Mrs.
Oswell."

"It's such a safeguard against crying. You
must let me come and see you when you're
in town ; I like you," she added suddenly.
"I wonder what our husbands are doing—I
hope Mr. Belcher will like Fred. Now, *that*
man, Mrs. Belcher, is simply an angel ; quali-
fied, I am thankful to say, with a few of the
weaknesses which apparently get worn out in

this charming world, so that there are none left for a future one."

"Is it a charming world?" Katherine asked, looking up at her with curiosity.

"Delightful. The people in it are so nice, occasionally bores, but kind, good creatures most of them, let that comfort you to reflect upon : it is the experience of someone a good deal older than yourself. There are exceptions, of course ; but it is a wise thing not to believe it, or else to think yourself the exception, and then you get along all right."

"I think," said Katherine, after a moment's pause, "you must be very happy."

"Yes, I'm very happy," Mrs. Oswell answered quickly. "I'm a woman, and married to the man I like best. I am strong and healthy and well, and live in a beautiful world, believing that the people in it mean well towards me and each other, and that if things go wrong it is merely an accident. And I have the art of being amused."

"Yes ; and you are not afraid of—anything," Katherine said, afraid of betraying too much.

"No, dear, of nothing," and Mrs. Oswell gave her companion's arm a sympathetic pinch. "My husband is an excellent companion, and has never been disagreeable for a minute. Of course, I pretend he has; I wouldn't let him know that he possessed the ghost of a virtue for the world, he'd be ashamed of it and try to live it down."

"I'm glad you said that about the world," Katherine said, not heeding the latter part of Mrs. Oswell's speech. "It makes me feel happier."

"Happiness is so often merely the result of one's own way of looking at things," Mrs. Oswell answered, while she thought to herself, "but if you find a way of looking at Mr. Belcher and getting any happiness out of it I shall be surprised."

The Oswells went on to Ambleside the next morning. Mrs. Oswell took her place on the top of the coach in high spirits, and

waved her hand to Katherine as they drove
away.

"A nice woman, Mrs. Oswell," Belcher repeated to his wife, "the sort of woman I like.
I wish you would learn to be lively, Katherine." She looked round at him with a smile
that came and went quickly, like a flash of
sunshine on still water.

"I'll try to be," she said as they walked
on. "You frighten me, sometimes," she went
on timidly, "but I want to be happy and to
make you so if I can—at any rate to please
you," she added, for it struck her that it
would be rather hopeless to try and make
so formidable a person as Mr. Belcher
happy.

"I shall let you know if you don't please
me," he said, with a sardonic smile. She
looked at him and hesitated before she found
courage to put the question that came to her
lips :

"Why did you marry me?" she asked.

"I thought I might as well, there wasn't

anyone else to do it, was there?" he said
mockingly.

"No." They walked along the road in
silence for a minute or two. Then she looked
up at him as if she were speaking aloud her
thoughts.

"I've been thinking about it all night," she
said gently. "We are married and have to be
together all our lives; but I feel as if I were
in your way. I don't think you like me very
much."

"Or that you like me very much?"

"No," she answered, raising her blue eyes
truthfully to his, and speaking reluctantly, "I
don't like you much, though I feel that I am
bound to you and cannot get away. I am too
much afraid of you—but I want to like you.
I wish we could be friends and companions
like Mr. and Mrs. Oswell."

"Well, you see you are not Mrs. Oswell,
and I'm not Mr. Oswell, and that makes a
difference. I'm afraid I can't talk sentiment,
Katherine; perhaps I shall when you are ten

years older, or someone else will for me. Meanwhile, here we are at the hotel. You had better go and walk about in the garden—I have some letters to answer."

"I'll go and see Dottel," she said, with a choke in her voice.

"Nuisance a schoolgirl is!" he said to himself. "She hasn't any flick. If she'd told me to go and be d——d I should have liked her."

Dottel was safely chained up in the yard, for he was a visitor not wholly appreciated by the hotel proprietor. She unfastened him and took him with her up a little pathway to a wooded knoll behind the hotel. The buds were showing themselves on the brown trees, and there were little clumps of primroses and violets in the underwood. She remembered the primroses she had tried to prevent Mr. Belcher from seeing in the garden at Shooter's Hill long ago, feeling that it would be sacrilege for his eyes to rest upon them; and she thought of Uncle Robert, who had gone by this time to some rooms in Bloomsbury; and

of Susan Barnes away in Somersetshire with
her own people ; and of Martyr. Poor stupid
Martyr ! He was lying deep in the muddy
Thames half-way between the Old Swan Pier
and North Woolwich. She remembered the
day when for the last time he had dragged
himself down the garden, and with half-blind
eyes, and feebly wagging tail, followed her
uncle and Mr. Belcher to Woolwich. They
carried with them two bricks and some string,
and they had to keep looking back and call-
ing Martyr to prevent him from turning home
again.   Mr. Belcher insisted on telling her, the
next time he came, how they had taken a little boat, and rowed out towards North Woolwich ; and then they had tied the brickbat
round Martyr's neck, put his head in a bag
and, midway across the river, lifted him over
the side of the boat. He seemed to take a
pleasure in her tears, and went on with a ma-
licious laugh that tortured her and made her
angry even now while she remembered it.   She
put her arms round a tree-trunk and drew up

closer to it, and told herself with strange un-
belief as though she doubted if it could be
true—that she was married to Mr. Belcher, and
had to spend all the years of her life with
him.

Then she looked at the blue lake beneath
and the great hills beyond, and was comforted.
The sunshine was sparkling on the water and
lighting up the streaks of snow on the moun-
tain-tops. "How beautiful it is," she said to
herself; "the whole world seems to be beautiful," and she remembered Mr. Oswell's account
of his travels and her talk afterwards with Mrs.
Oswell. "I should like to walk all over it
—alone. Perhaps some day when I am older
Edward will be different and take me to Italy,
only," and the tears rushed into her eyes, "I
should like so much better to go alone."

CHAPTER IV.

"THAT'S over," Mr. Belcher said as they took their places in the train at Windermere. "Rather waste of time—don't you think so, Katherine?—going on a honeymoon, eh?"

"I suppose people always go away when they are married?"

"Just as they do a great many other stupid things. Perhaps we shall get on a little better when we don't get quite so much of each other. I think marriage is rather a mistake, don't you?"

She was silent for a moment, then gathered courage to answer.

"Sometimes I think life is rather a mistake; but perhaps that is because I want so many things."

" What more do you want than what you have got ? "

" I don't know," she said with a puzzled look.

" That's just it—you don't know."

" Sometimes I feel as if I were not even inside the world, but only on the edge of it," she answered, forgetting for the moment that she was talking to Mr. Belcher, "and not inside life but only in a dream of it."

" Been reading novels ? " he asked with a little sneer.

" No," she answered, and put out her hand and touched his for a moment. " Don't laugh at me, Edward, and let me tell you things, being married makes me feel that I belong to you. I do so want you to—to——"

" All in good time," he said, and giving her finger a not unfriendly shake, took up his paper. She sat and looked out of window for an hour or two, and wondered what the house in Montague Place would be like. After all, she could not help the instincts of her sex, and

she was almost elated, for was she not going to
live in London a married woman and be the
mistress of a house? She would sit at the head
of the table and order the dinner every day—
at least, she supposed so ; she determined that
everything should be very punctual and
dainty. She wondered what the house was
like ; it would be easy to make the rooms look
pretty ; and she indulged in some visions of
elementary decorations such as Mrs. Barrett
had delighted in and her uncle had looked
upon with disapproval.

The day was closing in when they arrived,
and the house looked black and grim in the
deepening twilight. Her heart beat quickly,
and she felt as if she were treading the future
when she entered the doorway. Two servants
were waiting in the hall, a sharp-faced old one
who had been with Mr. Belcher's mother, and
a young one who was evidently kept in sub-
jection under her.

"Glad to see you, ma'am," the old one
said. "I am Gibson, at your service, I'm

sure; and this is Harriet," nudging the young
one, "and if she has faults she'll do her best.
Walk in, Sir, glad to see you back. No, cab-
man," she cried in a shrill voice, "we don't
let any of them people come in carrying boxes.
My nephew will do that, he's here on purpose," and she darted forward, thin and quick
like a gnat, while Katherine entered the dining-room and looked round it wonderingly.

A fire was blazing, and there was a lamp
burning on the sideboard—a lamp that had no
shade on it and brought out clearly the colour
of the red flock paper on the walls. The table
was laid for two, with great spaces of white
cloth that made it look desolate; and in the
centre was a large old-fashioned cruet-stand.
On the mantelpiece was a big marble clock,
and behind it a looking-glass that reached
nearly to the ceiling. The room was ugly,
with no attempt at decoration, and had but
few signs that it was lived in, yet it was fairly
comfortable and solid-looking—a certain sense
of dignity hung about it in spite of the red

6

flock paper. Katherine thought of the trees at Severndroog, and the scrubs, the gorse and blackberry bushes, and the garden of the White House. They had all gone out of her life for ever. Then she looked round the room in which she stood again, and felt that it might come to feel like home if only the human beings who ruled her life would have it so. She caught the reflection of her own face in the glass ; there was a smile upon it, for life is a wonderful thing with its fascinations and promises and the great silence that we call the future before us ; and she was young and curious.

Mr. Belcher followed her into the room and went towards a heap of letters she had not noticed on the sideboard. He opened one and began to read it.

"Oh," she exclaimed joyfully, going quickly to his side, " perhaps there are some for me."

" There are," he answered : " I am reading one from your uncle."

She looked at him in silence ; surely there was some mistake ; she took up the envelope— it was directed to her. She put her hand on the other letters and picked out a second one directed to her.

" Please let me open it," she said gently.

" You may open that," he nodded. " I wanted to see what your uncle said." He looked up for a moment and saw her face. " A man has a right to open his wife's letters," he said, " but she must not open his—you understand."

" I do so like opening them myself," she pleaded.

" I may so like opening them myself, and shall if it suits me," he laughed. " There ! there's your letter ; I've done with it. The old fool has been writing to Australia ; a brilliant idea has occurred to him that Richard may have married and left some children. I hope he didn't ; it would make a good deal of difference to us. Who's that from ? " he asked, looking at the letter in her hand.

"It is from Susan."

"Susan? Oh, the old woman who couldn't manage to die even with the help of a three months' illness—I don't want to read her letters. What do you think of the house? It belonged to Taylor the stockbroker, but he couldn't afford it after the crash in American railways some years ago, so I got it pretty cheaply: rather a good stroke of business? You had better go upstairs and take off your things," he said, with the quiet masterful manner that directed her every movement. "I wrote and ordered dinner yesterday, so I suppose it is nearly ready. Harriet will show you the way," and he rang the bell.

Then Harriet appeared with a flat candlestick and conducted Katherine up the desolate stone staircase.

Mr. Belcher went back to his letters. "Morris is an old fool," he thought. "Of course, if they know that he is looking for them, half-a-dozen brats will turn up and call themselves Richard's. I ought to have insisted

on a settlement; I may have saddled myself
with this girl for nothing at all. If she
wasn't to have Morris's money, I might just
as well have gone on amusing myself with
Florence. There's some life in her, and not
too much sentiment. I'm tired of this girl
following me about with her eyes that fill
with tears every time I choose to pinch her
hard enough." It was odd how much Katherine's slim figure and young face annoyed him.
He liked a full-blooded, well-developed woman
with slow gait and full deep voice, who expected everything and took it as a matter of
course or with a scornful laugh, and insulted
him openly. Besides, he had never thought
women worth looking at till they were eight-
and-twenty; by that time they had learnt to
know their way about and how to use their
tongues. He hated soft words, and despised
obedience even though he exacted it. Youth
and innocence were in his way; he liked to
hurt it, to see it writhe and shrink from him.
He had married Katherine with his eyes open,

of course, but with a clear and definite reason. Besides, it had seemed a natural incident enough. It was time he took a wife if he meant to take one at all, and in theory he had liked the idea of a young one: women were for flirtation, but girls were for marriage. Girls did not want equality and independence of thought and companionship, and all the modern nonsense that women were noisily struggling for nowadays. The nonsense was all very well to talk about, with other men's wives or a woman you had no intention of marrying, but a sensible man took care to exclude it rigorously from the daily experience of his own home. There he should be master and the first and only consideration, and so Mr. Belcher meant it to be in Montague Place.

"I'm going out," he said to Katherine after dinner. "I want to talk to your uncle."

"May I go with you? I should so like to see Uncle Robert's new rooms."

"I want to talk to him alone," he answered. "You had better do your unpacking to-morrow," he went on, always careful to arrange her time as far as possible, "and go to bed at ten. To-morrow you can set about helping Gibson with the housekeeping."

"I think I can do it by myself after a bit," she said timidly. "I did it at home when Susan was ill."

"Gibson knows my ways," he answered.

He walked quickly towards Gower Street. At one of the houses near University College Mr. Morris had taken rooms.

He was at home, the servant said. Mr. Belcher walked quickly upstairs to the first floor. The door of the drawing-room was opened by a tall woman of about eight-and-thirty. She was dressed in black, and round her neck there was a crucifix; she looked imperious, but her manner was that of one who had been executing an errand.

"Ah," she said, and her accent betrayed that she was a Frenchwoman of somewhat limited English. "You want Monsieur Morris? *Le voici.*" Mr. Belcher looked at her

with astonishment. She motioned him into
the room and, shutting the door, disappeared.

"Who was the good lady kindly qualify-
ing your solitude?" he inquired. Mr. Morris
was sitting by the fire in an arm-chair.

"She is a—a widowed sister-in-law of Mrs.
Merrick, who keeps this house. She lives
here."

"I see."

"How is Katherine?"

"She's all right. Do you like these
rooms?"

"I don't think I shall stay in them long; I
want to get into the country again."

"You'll be better there," Mr. Belcher answered, "and safer," he thought, for a Frenchwoman about the place was an unexpected
turn in affairs. "I have been thinking," he
went on aloud, "that it's hardly fair I should
have the entire burden of Katherine's main-
tenance. I always expected that you would
make some definite settlement on her during
your lifetime."

Mr. Morris looked up sharply, and was silent for a moment before he answered. "It's customary for a man to maintain his wife," he said. "However, when you pay me back that four thousand, I'll settle it upon her at once."

"You see," continued Belcher, without noticing the remark, "I married her chiefly because you wished it; I believe you thought it some compensation for the money I owed you?"

"It was your own idea, and as for my wishes, you married her because you thought it time to get married, and because I told you that as Richard was dead I should leave what I had to her. It is not so much as it would have been if things had turned out as you led me to expect."

"A will is not a very good security for a promise."

"You'll get no other," Mr. Morris answered positively, "and if, as Madame Quiblier, the lady who left the room as you entered, suggested to me a day or two ago,

Richard has left a wife or children, I shall make a fresh disposition of my property."

"That idea about Richard is all nonsense; of course, if you make known in Melbourne that you are seeking for grandchildren in order to endow them, why every house in Collins Street will produce some. However, if you like I will advertise in the Australian papers?"

Mr. Morris looked at him carefully again. "I think I can manage to do that myself, thank you."

"It might be amusing to go out there and see what it is like ; perhaps if you wait a few months we could go together."

"We'll see," Mr. Morris answered brusque-ly. "Go home to your wife, Belcher, that's the best place for you," and he held out his hand.

Belcher felt himself dismissed as cava-lierly as he in turn treated Katherine. "I shall have to keep a good hold upon him," he thought as he went back. "Or with the

Frenchwoman on one side and Richard's foundlings on the other he'll make a nice mess of it. He's as obstinate as the devil, but a woman might influence him. I wish I had left marriage alone: it is only amusing for the first week."

CHAPTER V.

MR. BELCHER suffered Katherine to live in his house, and was civil to her. He even recognised that she had a right to be there, but he took no trouble to make her life pleasant; and at the end of six months she knew him little better than she had done at the end of three. He consulted her about nothing, told her nothing. She had virtually no share in household matters; Gibson saw to those, and kept a sharp eye on everything—including Katherine, whom she did not view too favourably. Day after day went by with unvarying monotony. Breakfast at eight; Katherine poured out the coffee while Mr. Belcher read his letters and the paper. When he had finished it, he looked up and made a few curt remarks, much as though she were an upper servant who was bound to stay with him. At nine he went out; at a little before seven he came back and generally inquired what she had done during the day, not with the interest of a husband who cared, but with the air of a taskmaster who found some gratification in knowing that the hours had been long and difficult. After dinner, he read his papers again or wrote letters. Once he tried to teach her the mysteries of double dummy, but, finding that she did not take a vivid interest in the game, he put the cards away with a curt, " I think we have had enough of that, thank you," and did not attempt it again. At ten o'clock he sent her to bed, and as she left the room she generally saw him reach down a box of cigars from a shelf in the corner, as though he meant to indulge in a pleasant hour after she had gone. This was in the dining-room, in which they always sat, for the drawing-room was covered up with dusting sheets and hidden from the light of day. There was a

little room on the stairs to which Katherine
went if she felt that her presence was not required by Mr. Belcher in the dining-room;
and he often made her feel that it was not
only not required, but in the way.

Mr. Morris spent the evening in Montague
Place occasionally, but his manner towards
her, though it was a little gentler, was not
more easy than formerly, and she knew that
he came to talk business with her husband,
and so left them together. Sometimes two or
three men came to dinner, and she sat silently
at the other end of the table; for Mr. Belcher
looked displeased if she talked, and told her
once in a sarcastic manner after they had gone
that her conversation was not of absorbing
interest: so she took the hint and remained
silent. A few people, wives of solicitors and
anxious barristers, called upon her, and she
returned their calls and there the acquaintance ended. Mrs. Oswell came now and then,
evidently out of kindness at first, and afterwards because she liked the lonely girl.

Katherine learnt many things from her : how to dress (though for that purpose Mr. Belcher gave her no money), and what to read, and a little of what was going on in the world. Thus in some dim fashion she began to understand things better, and gained as much wisdom, perhaps, as it is given to unsophisticated girlhood to know.

"She ought to read the modern people," Mr. Oswell said ; and his wife lent her Tennyson and Browning and Swinburne. They left her with the sense that had so often beset her since her marriage—a sense that life had cheated her ; that she stood by the gate of the world, but Mr. Belcher held her back and would not let her go through and take her share of the chances beyond.

Now and then during the first months he was good-natured after his own fashion. He took her to a theatre two or three times, more to amuse himself with her surprise at what she saw than to give her pleasure. Once he took her to Brighton from Saturday to Monday, but he met someone he knew and neglected her, and when he went again he left her at home, and she was glad enough of the three days in silence and without him. She was never at ease with him, never for a single hour, for though her fear of him grew less as time went on, her dislike of him increased, until it woke up every nerve and sense in her to shrink from his touch, from the sound of his voice, the mere fact of his presence. The one comfort of her life was that he went out every day and all day. After a time he often went out in the evening too. She never knew where he went or what he did ; he gave no hint of his doings, and she never dreamt of asking him for any account of them.

But gradually she created a life for herself ; a life of books and thought, and long walks, and voyages of discovery into the far depths of London. She made little attempts, too, at helping others who were poorer than herself ; but she had no money for these last, and so in despair had to hold aloof. Some of her in-

nocence vanished, some of her simplicity. She
knew perfectly why Mr. Belcher had married
her, and the half-contempt with which he re-
garded her. Sometimes she tried to soften
him, to win his regard or admiration, but it
was only done as a matter of duty or in recognition of the fact that she was his wife, and
with almost a dread of her efforts having any
success. Books had taught her the possibilities that the world holds for each man or
woman who comes into it, and she looked on
aghast at the trick that fate had played her.
She guessed keenly enough what they were
like, those happinesses and miseries that are
but the complement of each other; and she
realised still more keenly the bondage that
was her own portion. In those lonely days,
too, there stirred in her heart for the first time
a definite longing for human sympathy and
companionship, and a breathless knowledge,
though she drove it from her as a forbidden
one, that in human love lay the secret of
human joy.

7

With all this, since she was but a mortal woman, there came a little undercurrent of happy vanity—for she was growing beautiful. Her eyes were more tender, and the sight of joy or sorrow that others carried, even though they were strangers to her, had altered the expression of her face.   Moreover, walking had made her figure lissom, and thrown back her shoulders so that she looked tall and supple.

"I should like to know the end of your history," Mrs. Oswell thought, as Katherine entered one afternoon, a glow of health on her face and the dimple in her cheek showing itself more frequently than formerly.   "It isn't Mr. Belcher, or I am much mistaken."   Then she said aloud : "Well, you look as if you had found your own two feet and stood on them."

"I have done more," Katherine answered, "for I have walked about the world on them, and looked at the people."

"Yes."

"And have come to the conclusion that everyone else is needed by some one. No one needs me—even Gibson thinks me in the way."

"Someone has need of you; that is why you were born. Only you have not found it out yet, and the world itself has need of you too: we are all little bits in the great mosaic."

"I don't like to think that," Katherine answered; "it sounds so hopeless; it is what a fatalist might say. I would rather be an atom of dust in the desert whirled along by all the winds that blow—and thankful that there are four of them—or a waif strayed by mistake into the wrong world."

"My dear, your husband has need of you." Mrs. Oswell said it from duty and tried to say it positively.

"No. I wish he had; then I wouldn't mind how badly he treated me." For she had long ceased to disguise her life from Mrs. Oswell, who had seen clearly what manner of man Mr. Belcher was from the first, though with easy good-nature she had tried to defend him. "He has only need of Uncle Robert's money."

Mrs. Oswell put her hand on Katherine's. "I don't believe in our lives being an atom of dust in the desert. Perhaps one day, my dear," she said gently, "you may have a little child."

"I hope not." Her cheeks flushed, and her eyes filled with tears. "If it were a boy, he might grow up to be like his father: I don't want to see more men in the world like Edward. If it were a girl, it might be as lonely as I have been, and make a marriage like mine."

"It would have a mother."

"Yes," Katherine answered, clasping her hands across her breast as if they held a little one in them, "and she would be powerless to help its life, and it would feel that she was useless and ignore her, or perhaps it would be sorry for her. I shouldn't like my child to be sorry for me," she went on, lifting her head. "I shouldn't like anyone in the world to be that, unless it was someone much stronger than myself—someone I loved."

"Ah!" exclaimed Mrs. Oswell, "now we are coming to it, and I can see the red light in the distance."

"The red light?"

"It means danger." Mrs. Oswell counted the gold bangles on her wrist. "My dear, why don't you make your husband fall in love with you?"

"My husband!" Katherine exclaimed with a shudder she could not hide. "I never see him except at breakfast time : he's out all day, and generally all the evening too now."

"You know," said Mrs. Oswell, forgetting her tact in her eagerness to be clever, "I shouldn't be at all surprised if there's some woman he's fond of and goes to spend his evenings with. You see he was six-and-thirty, rather more, when he married you : a man doesn't get to that age for nothing, and he wasn't in love with you, dear ; that was plain enough on your honeymoon."

"And plain enough every moment he has been with me since," Katherine answered bitterly. But there gathered a little fire at her heart, a little fierceness that increased her hatred of Mr. Belcher as she thought of the possibility of his having cared for someone else, perhaps all the years of his life, and of the manner in which he possibly spent his evenings while she sat alone in Montague Place. It put a sense of insult into her life that had not been there before.

"Mrs. Oswell," she said, and burst into tears, "it's a terrible thing to be a woman."

"Would you like to be a man?"

"I wouldn't for the wide world," she answered, with a little horror in her voice.

"Would you like to be a horrid strong-minded thing clamouring for rights?"

"Of course not," Katherine said indignantly. "I don't think I know what I want, really."

"You'll find out one day," Mrs. Oswell answered. "And when you do," she thought,

"I wonder whether it will be a comedy or a tragedy."

"I think I'll go away," Katherine said. "I have found out a strange pleasure in life," she added, turning to Mrs. Oswell with the quick smile that was a fascination. "It is walking about London looking at the people. Everyone lives a separate life and has a separate soul and experiences and secrets, and hopes and ambitions, some of which I know and others at which I only guess. I like to see two people together best, and to notice how they behave to each other. The most interesting are a man and a woman together."

"You have arrived at that fatal knowledge, have you?" said Mrs. Oswell.

"I think," Katherine went on, not heeding her, "it must be the most beautiful thing in the world to be the woman and to love the man, if he is strong and handsome and clever and everything in the world, and if he loves you back again."

"My dear," laughed Mrs. Oswell, "I wish

you could love your husband. A woman can
love the strangest thing in mankind if only the
whim takes her. For Heaven's sake, go home
and get sentimental on Mr. Belcher. It's my
sincere opinion that if you don't you'll come
to utter grief somehow and some day when
you find out that every woman alive is blessed
or cursed with a heart."

"I am different," said Katherine. "I have
only a little bit of one, but I am very lonely.
I think my rôle is to walk about the world
and look at it, but not to play any part.
Sometimes I feel like a crane I used to know
when I was a little girl: it stood on one leg
contemplating the moat by Eltham Palace.
Only I don't want to stand still as that did : I
should like to walk from one end of the world
to the other, it is such a beautiful place."

"And such a sad one."

"Yes, perhaps. Mrs. Oswell, you have
been very kind to me; I am very grateful
and would love you for it if I could, but I
don't think I know how. They didn't teach

me in the days of my youth. Good-bye ; it's nearly four o'clock and time to go home. Dottel will be back."

"And your husband too ? "

"No, he sends Dottel back by the office boy."

"And goes off to spend his evenings elsewhere," thought Mrs. Oswell. "Depend upon it he doesn't spend them alone nor always with his own sex; a man's vanity prevents him from doing that." Katherine was looking round the room : she knew by an instinct that had been born in her that its colours were incongruous, its nick-nacks too many, its effects crude and perhaps a little vulgar, but still it showed that the woman of the house had a voice in it, arranged her furniture as she pleased, and took a pleasure in her home.

"I wish I had a home," she said.

"My dear child, you have!" Mrs. Oswell exclaimed, almost startled.

"No. Mr. Belcher has a home, and lets me stay in it, but I have no business there. I should like a room to decorate and make pretty, and that my husband would come home and admire. You said that everyone in the world was needed by some one person. Perhaps everyone in the world has a home somewhere, but some go on and on and never find it, or die before they reach it."

"But there is a little room you sometimes sit in alone," Mrs. Oswell said; "why don't you make that pretty?"

"I have no money. Uncle Robert gave me a present at Christmas, but I spent it on beggars and clothes."

"Doesn't Mr. Belcher give you any? What do you do for postage-stamps?"

"Put them down in the weekly books; but I don't use two a month," she laughed. "Good-bye again. I must go back to Mr. Belcher's house. I wish you hadn't said that about another woman: it makes me shrink from him a little more. I believe some morning I shall run away."

"And what will you do then?"

She looked back as she went out of the doorway. " Walk all over the world, seeking——"

"Seeking what?"

"I don't know yet—but I shall." ·

" She is like a woman in a dream," Mrs. Oswell said to her husband that night. " Poor little soul, I wish she would wake up."   .

" Humph ! Perhaps she is better off in the dream ."

" Perhaps—oh, Fred, dear, what a blessing you are ! I feel as if I ought to say grace over you, thanking God for my good husband as children sometimes thank Him for their good dinner."

"I don't think we have a bad time on the whole——"

" We have a splendid time," she answered.

CHAPTER VI.

It was nearly Easter. Katherine had been married more than a year. The buds were on the trees again : there was blue in the sky, and the sun was shining. The streets were full of flower-sellers. People loitered as they walked, looking in at the shops—or stayed in the park to watch the carriages driving quickly along—the faces in them looked as though they had been told a secret that was pleasant.

"I know what it is," Katherine said to herself. "they may look old, but they feel young. Spring has touched their hearts, the sunshine is in their eyes and they see how lovely it is. I wish Edward——" But as she thought of him there came back the memory of his jibes

and his mocking tone, his visible intolerance
of her presence. "I wish I could disappear
out of his life. I am like a prisoner at the end
of a chain that lets me go out a little way, just
so far, and never any farther." She stopped,
as she went along Oxford Street, at a flower-
stall. There were bunches of daffodils, round
balls of them, each with a few green blades in
the centre.

"Twopence a bunch, miss," the man said.
She had a shilling of her own, and walked
back to Montague Place with her arms full of
flowers. People looked at her as she passed
them by. Her dark hair was coiled up into
a knot, her grey-blue eyes looked fearlessly
ahead, as if into the future. She had the expression of a woman who is waiting and knows
that she has far to go before she reaches her
goal. But her face had grown more content.
The beauty of the world appealed to her so
strongly that her own life seemed too trivial
a thing to consider over much. Besides, she
felt that even that trivial thing, her own life,

belonged to the world far more than to Mr. Belcher. "I shall live in the world all my days, whether I am with him or not, and be buried in it when I die," she thought. He did not want her, though between them there was the terrible fetter of marriage—that she hated and at which he chafed, but that neither of them could break. "For only death or sin could undo marriage, no matter how blindly it was entered upon or how miserable it proved," she thought hopelessly.

"A handsome girl," a man said to his wife as they passed her.

"Beautiful," answered the woman.

Katherine heard them ; a smile came to her lips and looked out of her eyes. "I wonder if it is true," she said to herself: "to be beautiful in a beautiful world sounds wonderful," and she went on her way. "I wish some giant would arrive," she thought, "and sweep all these houses into the sea, and we could devise some way of living without them, under trees or in tents. If we could wander away to the far ends of the world just as we liked, how much better it would be. Then Edward would not sit in an office all day and listen to quarrels and grievances, and he would think some good of human nature, just as Mrs. Oswell does, and he wouldn't care for money—he would be altogether different. Perhaps his office is very ugly, and the peo-ple who go to him are mean and ugly too : trying to get money may have made them so, and they reflect themselves in him. He may have been quite different when he started in life"—she was turning the key in the door of Montague Place, and entered with her daffodils. " If he would only be different again ! I shouldn't fall in love with him as Mrs. Oswell said, but I should like to admire him and to think how good he was, and that it was all my fault if we were not happy to-gether."

He was going to dine at home that evening, so she arranged some daffodils for the table, wondering if they would please him ; but it was a forlorn hope, she had made the place pretty with flowers before and looked her best at dinner and tried all the artifices that youth and prettiness know—only to find them useless. He had seen through them, and showed her that he did, and gone out. It was four o'clock when the flowers were done: two or three hours yet before he came home. An idea crossed her mind and took possession of her. "I'll go and see Uncle Robert," she said; "it's just possible I may find him in, and it is a long time since I saw him." As if she had been touched by a finger of fate, she turned and went out of the house. She had only been to see him once or twice before since he had come to town, she never understood what hurried her to him now. The Frenchwoman opened the door and looked radiant.

"Oh, this is good!" she cried; "I am glad that you have come; there is great news. Go upstairs, madame, and let monsieur your uncle tell you himself."

The sitting-room was in a state of chaos.

Mr. Morris was packing some papers into a box ; he looked at her with a moment's silent bewilderment before he spoke.

"Katherine"—his voice was eager and hurried—"I did not expect you. Why have you come? I have not told Belcher yet."

"What has happened, Uncle Robert?" she asked. "Are you going away?" He looked at her under his eyebrows while he answered in the old hard manner that he only seemed to maintain with a struggle.

"I had a letter to-day by the Australian mail. Richard—my son, has left a wife and two boys. I go to Liverpool to-morrow, and sail for Melbourne on Wednesday."

"I am glad. Oh! dear Uncle Robert, I'm very glad."

"Belcher won't be," he said shortly; "he'll think that I shall not leave you so much money."

"What does it matter? People seem to buy wickedness and misery with money. Perhaps these children will make you happy."

8

"But what will your husband say?" She stopped and considered; a shudder passed through her.

"I don't know," she answered, and quailed a little.

"I did not know he was so hard, Katherine, or I would not have let you marry him. I thought I was doing the best I could for you. A woman is better married, and there was no one else." It was the only apology he could bring himself to make, and he made it grudgingly.

"Perhaps he doesn't mean——" she began.

"I'm glad you have come," Mr. Morris went on, not heeding her, "for I wanted to give you this; I wrote it out, and have been wondering how to get it to you without his knowledge. It is a cheque for two hundred pounds. If I should not return, and he treats you badly, it will help you to do something or bring you out to Australia. Perhaps you had better cash it to-morrow; it is not crossed;

go to the bank, get notes, and keep them by
you."

"Oh, Uncle Robert, could you not take
me with you? He does not want me, indeed——"

"Nonsense! A woman's place is with her
husband," he said, with his old curtness, and
she knew there was no appeal. "I must have
a talk with Belcher; there is a great deal to
say to him before I go. I'll come and dine
with you to-night. You had better go back
now. Tell him I shall be there by half-past
seven—and, Katherine, get that cheque cashed
to-morrow, but don't spend the money unless
you're obliged. Stay! Can you take this
telegram for me? I must tell them to keep a
room for me to-morrow night at the hotel at
Liverpool, or I may find myself stranded; I
sail on Wednesday morning. Now, good-
bye." He looked at her for a moment, and
the expression of his face softened. "You
have grown into a handsome girl," he said;
"the Frenchwoman downstairs talks a good

deal of nonsense about you, but I believe she's right." He put his hands upon her shoulder and kissed her forehead. That was his farewell, for, though he came to dinner that night, she did not see him alone again. She asked if she might see him off from Euston, but he refused, though he seemed pleased at the request.

CHAPTER VII.

MR. BELCHER hardly spoke to Katherine that evening while her uncle was there, and the next morning he seemed too much engrossed with his own thoughts even to ·be aware of her presence ; but he looked back with an expression that frightened her as he left the house. It was the day Mr. Morris left London ; she knew that he had some business with her husband in the middle of the day, and that was all.

The storm burst at dinner. He hardly spoke till the cloth was cleared and Harriet had left the room.

"Your uncle is probably in Liverpool by this time," he said.

"I know," she said, feeling that there was more to come.

"And has left me saddled with you for the rest of my days."

"I am sorry, but it is not my fault," she said, and stood facing him on the hearth-rug.

"If you had been a clever woman you would have managed him. You haven't a spark of cleverness in you. The result is that he has made a totally inadequate provision for you, and, if this woman and her brats get over him, he'll probably make it worse still. I suppose he calls that behaving like an honest man. I don't. An old fool—he was always an old fool!"

"Please don't say that to me," she said gently. "I am sorry he has gone, and I hope he will find his grandchildren. They will make him happier."

"Bosh! I hate sentiment. I wonder if you know how tired I am of seeing you, Katherine. I only married you because Morris wanted to get rid of you."

"He didn't," she flashed. He looked at

her for a moment and tried to cow her with a
still more bullying manner.

"He wanted to get rid of you, and there
was no other way of doing it. He was tired
of you, as I am."

"Why did you marry me? You knew
that I did not want you, and you were not
obliged to do it; and you didn't do it because
you liked me, but only because you thought
you would get money by it. Oh! I hate
money; I hate nothing in the world so much
as money. But now that is done," she went
on quickly, with a tremble in her voice, "what
is the good of making me miserable? I have
done nothing that I knew would vex you since
I've come into the house. Why can't you be
kind to me?"

"I don't want to be kind to you. I know
that you dislike me, and I dislike you, wandering up and down the house with your soft
footsteps like a cat. You are just like a cat!"

"Why do you say such cruel things to
me? I have done nothing to make you hate

me so much. Is it because you like anybody
else?" she asked, remembering Mrs. Oswell's
unwise remark.

"Yes, I like someone else," he answered
triumphantly, "and always have. Somebody
who has plenty to say, and is quick and merry,
and doesn't bore one as you do."

"Why didn't you marry her?" she asked
scornfully.

"She was married, and found her husband
as great a clog as I find a wife; but now he's
dead—he died six months ago—and she is
free, and I always hated girls: they are so
stupid."

"And I hate you," she cried, "more than
anything in the world. You married me for
money, and I'm glad you have not got it. I
hope you will never get any, and I shall write
and tell Uncle Robert so."

"You can write him anything you please.
He has gone to the devil, and I wish you
would go after him. I saw Williams, the
doctor, this afternoon, and he said that the

chances are nineteen to twenty against his re-
turning alive; and he did his worst, as far as
you are concerned, before he started to-day."

She turned to leave the room without another word.

"This has been a nice little scene," he said.

"Oh!" she said, and burst into tears, "will
nothing set us free? I never wanted to marry
you, and you have never cared for me; it is
frightful to think that we are condemned to
be together all our lives. Couldn't we part—
or at least try to be a little better towards
each other?" She unconsciously held out
her hand as if in pacification. With uncon-
trollable rage he struck it away.

"Get out!" he said, opening the door; "I
am sick and tired of the sight of you, and
have no patience with tears." She looked at
her hand unbelievingly and at him, then
walked slowly away. He heard her going
upstairs. He stood still for a moment. "I
wonder why I hate her so much. Some men
would like her—she is growing handsome. I

believe I hate her because she doesn't fight me.
I like a spice of the devil in a woman."

Katherine went into the little room she
called her own. It was still gay with daffodils. She threw herself down on the sofa. A
corner as of something sharp made itself felt
against her chest; she put up her hand to it
and remembered. It was the bank-notes into
which she had changed her uncle's cheque.

She came down early the following morning, for sleep was impossible. The bitterness
and insult of the quarrel last night had stag-
gered her; she shivered as she entered the
dining-room. There were two letters by her
plate on the breakfast table; the top one was
addressed in Susan's handwriting, the other
she did not know. She slipped them quickly
into her pocket, for she knew that Mr. Belcher
would jeer at them even if he did not read
them. She heard him coming, and put her
hand to her throat for a moment to steady
herself.

"Good morning," he said, in the mocking voice that always made her writhe; "slept well?" She looked back at him with the clear, unflinching expression that provoked his admiration.

"Yes, I slept well," she said. "It was happiness to sleep, for I forgot everything." Her manner was distant, but so oddly courteous that for a moment he was puzzled. She stood looking at him, tall and scornful yet polite, older by five years than when he had married her, although it was only fifteen months ago.

"In a temper?"

"No," she answered calmly. "Perhaps we'd better have breakfast." She poured out his coffee and put it beside him, with his paper. There were some minutes of silence, then he looked up.

"I think we arrived at a full understanding last night," he said. "If you had been a clever woman you would have wheedled your uncle out of some money."

"I did not want it."

"There'll be next to nothing now when he dies—that is, if he gets out there safely and finds these brats. I should not wonder if he makes a new will, and does away with the little he has left you. He'll probably stay out there. He has resigned his directorship and everything else. Meanwhile, I'm saddled with a log in the shape of a woman all my life. I thought he was going to leave you twenty-five thousand pounds, Katherine." She got up and poked the fire.

"I'm glad you are not going to get it."

"Glad, are you?" he exclaimed, starting up and staring at her face.

"Yes, glad!" she cried. "You have made me miserable. I'm glad you are not going to get his money."

"You fool!" he exclaimed, and raised his hand and struck her again, just as when she was a child, and before he had grown more gentle, her Uncle Robert used to strike her. She turned, and looked at him with a face so

white and terrible that he was frightened. She
put her hand upon the bell; he seized it and
pulled it away. "Go and sit down," he said,
and almost pushed her back into her place.
"Will you never understand that I was hood-
winked into marrying you—a schoolgirl I
don't care twopence about—thinking you
would have what you never will have? I've
not wanted to be unkind to you," he said
half apologetically, "but it makes me so
impatient to think that I am tied to a dummy, a fool, a log, a mill-stone; and marriage is so interminable." She got up again,
and stood on the same spot where he had
struck her.

"I don't want it to go on," she said. "You
made me marry you. I was a baby, and did
not dare oppose you and Uncle Robert. But
it is not marriage," she said with sudden bitterness; "it's not like the Oswells' marriage,
or the marriage of the men and women I see
walking about. You have never been kind to
me, and you have given me no sympathy or

companionship since the day we started from Shooter's Hill together."

"I've given it elsewhere."

"You have only insulted me and made me miserable," she went on calmly, not noticing his remark. "Why must we go on living together? I know you hate me, as I do you. My one desire is to go out of your sight forever. Let me go!"

"You can go to the devil, if you like," he said. And he thought, "She's uncommonly good-looking, and I had no idea that there was so much spirit in her. Perhaps, after all, she's only artful, and not such a fool as I took her to be."

"Let me go," she repeated, "and live with Susan in Somersetshire, or in one of the little cottages beyond the churchyard at Eltham." And she thought of the palace and the crane.

"Who's to pay for the separate establishment, I should like to know? It might, of course, be amusing to go and see you in a cottage," he sneered ; "it would make you seem less like a wife—a wife is such a bore. I could run down and dine with you sometimes. I never understood why people should be forced to live together all their days, and every day, just because they're married. If you lived in the next street, we should not hate each other so much."

"If you would only let me go," she went on, not heeding his remark. "I could live on very little money."

"I don't choose you to go away. Your precious uncle would certainly do nothing for you then."

Gibson opened the door and looked in.

"Your portmanteau is ready, sir."

"Send for a hansom." Then he spoke to Katherine again. "I am going out of town for a few days. This is Wednesday—the day your precious uncle goes on board at Liverpool. I shall be away over Easter. If you hadn't been a fool I might have taken you with me; as it is, I shall get pleasanter company. When I return we'll continue our ami-

able relations. I'll put two pounds on the
mantelpiece in case you want any money while
I'm away; you can keep an account of it."
He opened the door. "Is the hansom there?"
he called.

"Yes, sir."

"Good-bye," he said, turning back to Katherine; "perhaps as we are going to be separated for a whole week we'd better kiss each
other."

"If you dare," she said scornfully, her
eyes flashing with anger. "I hate you—I
hate you—I hate you! I would rather be
bitten by a tiger or stung—anything in the
world rather than let you touch me. Go
away, go away!" He stood and looked at
her for a moment with amazement. Gibson
came to the door.

"Your bag's on the top, sir," she said.

He looked at Katherine again and laughed.

"You did that very well," he said, and
went out of the house followed by Gibson.
"If she were always like that," he thought,

as he drove off, "she'd be something like. I begin to think she's rather amusing, after all."

The hansom drove away. Gibson came up the steps, and closed the dining-room door as she passed. Then Katherine walked up and down trying to get calm. "I can't bear it," she cried to herself, "I can't go on bearing it. I would rather die than live like this. Uncle Robert sails to-day"—she stopped and considered. "But there would be no time to overtake him at Liverpool; he may have started already. I'll telegraph to him," and she went to the writing-table by the window; "but no, it would be no good. Oh!" and with a sense of insult that was not to be borne, she put her hands against the side of her face that he had struck. "I cannot—cannot live and see him again; I must go away somewhere. Uncle Robert gave me the money—he surely gave it me for this. I'll follow him out"— but as she said it a feeling of despair came over her, and she shook her head. "He

9

wouldn't understand," she said; "he used— he used"—she hesitated, for she could not bear to remember unkindness after so many years—"he used to strike me, too, when I was little. He thinks about women as Edward does—that they should have no feeling but submission towards men, and take even blows with meekness." It was the old idea, she thought. But men were not like it in these days, or only the few, and they the second-rate men, who were afraid of being found out if they did not protect themselves with tyranny. The best men of any class were different. She knew that it was so. She had seen Mr. and Mrs. Oswell and all the people who walked together in the streets of London. Little Harriet downstairs was miserable for months after her father died, and her mother had nearly died, too, of a broken heart. No one would die of a broken heart for Mr. Belcher. "Oh, I can't bear it! I can't bear it!" she cried, and hid her face in her hands. "I will go away—right away—and never let him see me

again. I will go to Susan and live with her."
Then she remembered that there was a letter
from Susan in her pocket, as well as another
in a strange hand—the letters she had found
on the table when she came down. Susan's
was merely to wish her a happy Easter, and
to say that she had not been well lately, and
had a niece coming to stay with her. Katherine read it first from a sense of loyalty, but
she was curious about the strange one : it
made a break in the misery of that terrible
morning. It proved to be from a firm of
solicitors in Chancery Lane, and enclosed a
cheque for ninety pounds, a legacy less duty,
bequeathed her by Mrs. Barrett, who had died
three months before. She looked up with
amazement, a little dulled by the excitement
she had been going through. Ninety pounds,
and no one knew she had it, besides the two
hundred her uncle had given her on Monday !
It was a fortune to Katherine, for she was
wholly unused to deal with money, and knew
but little of its value. It was surely a chance

sent from Heaven? If only Mrs. Oswell were
in town she would have gone to consult her;
as it was, she sat still with clasped hands
looking at the cheque. It was crossed and
payable to order. "I will go to the bank
and cash it, and then I'll go to Bridgwater
to Susan and have one happy peaceful week
before he comes back, and then—he shall come
and fetch me if he wants me. Poor Susan!
if she is ill I can nurse her," she thought,
longing to be tender to somebody. "She will
be glad when she sees me. I cannot stay. I
must go—I must; and it is best for both of
us. I cannot, cannot stay!" she kept on re-
peating to herself as she went slowly upstairs
and, like a woman in a dream, gathered together most of her belongings. "I had better
take them. I shall never come back unless
he makes me," she thought; "perhaps Susan
will like them when I am dead." She pulled
her trunk, the one she had taken to Windermere, out from the corner. The lock was
broken; it did not matter; there was a little

strap on either side that would be fastening enough. She began putting in one thing after another till it was full, hardly knowing what she did, only eager to get away from the house, away from Mr. Belcher for ever and ever. She took Uncle Robert's money out of the little desk in which she had hidden it last night, and put it in her bosom, and then she looked at the cheque for Mrs. Barrett's legacy. "I wonder if she knows about me now," she said to herself, "or if the dead know nothing, but lie in their graves straight and still for ever." She went to the glass to put on her hat and stared at her own face. It was like a stranger's. Then she wandered aimlessly round the room, as if trying to remember something. "No, no; that is all." She sighed and rang the bell.

"Harriet," she said, "send for a cab and have this box put on it. I am going to Bridg-water."

Gibson came up quickly.

"Does the master know you were going,

ma'am ?" he asked sharply; "and when are you coming back ? "

"That does not concern you, Gibson," Katherine answered quietly; "Mr. Belcher will be here on Wednesday; you had better be ready for him." The box was put on the cab, and she drove away. The two servants looked at each other.

"He's kept too tight a hand," Gibson said to herself, "just as his father did before him. It's my belief she's gone away to cry her life out with that old woman at Bridgwater."

"If I was in her place," thought Harriet, "I wouldn't come back till I couldn't help myself. He doesn't care a bit about her. Lor! she should have seen father and mother and what they was to each other."

CHAPTER VIII.

KATHERINE held her breath as she drove away. She felt like a prisoner escaping, and prayed that she might never enter the house again ; to live in it meant misery and degradation. A change must be made ; something must happen. She would go to Susan, go anywhere—what did it matter where ?—for the rest of her days. She was cowed and insulted, miserable and desperate.

"But I will never go back," she said to herself, "I will never, never enter the house again. Uncle Robert's money and Mrs. Barrett's legacy shall save me. I had better get the cheque cashed at once. Oh, dear Mrs. Barrett, thank you, thank you for leaving it to me." At the bank she learnt to her surprise that they could not change it, and the clerk explained the mystery of the two lines across it.

"But I have no banking account," she said.

"Then the simplest way would be to take it back to the drawers," he suggested, "their office is only at the top of Chancery Lane, not a hundred yards from here."

"Thank you," she said, and gave the clerk a grateful look: he remembered it all that day.

The lawyers readily agreed to cash the cheque for her, and when she had signed it and some strange mark had been put upon it, a messenger was sent to the bank. "I saw your husband yesterday, Mrs. Belcher," the senior partner remarked.

"Yes? He was to go to the country this morning," she answered, with a little shudder she could not help.

"And are you about to follow him?" he asked politely.

"No, I'm going to a friend of my own at Bridgwater."

"I often saw him at Brighton during the winter."

"Yes, he went from Saturday till Monday," and she remembered how she had been left at home—though she had been thankful enough to be at peace—while he had possibly been with somebody else, the somebody else he liked so much, and who was now free. Surely she was right to go away? She must and would—and for ever.

"You have only twenty minutes to catch your train," the lawyer said, as he handed her the notes and saw her down to her cab. "I wonder what made that beautiful girl marry Belcher?" he thought as she disappeared. "I wouldn't give much for her chance of happiness, poor thing. I have a notion somehow that he doesn't know about this little legacy, and I shall not feel it my duty to enlighten him."

Meanwhile, Katherine drove on to Paddington. "I feel as if I carried a fortune," she thought, but she was cold and sick with misery,

for Mr. Belcher's blow haunted her, and fear—
the fear that somehow he would overtake her
even before she reached the shelter of Susan's
little home at Bridgwater.   This was why she
did not realise till the porter opened the cab
door that she was at least five minutes too late
for. her train.

"I must wait for the next," she said.

By some accident her box slipped as it was
being lifted from the cab and fell on to the
pavement; the broken lock gave way, the lid
was twisted aside and one of the hinges
wrenched from its bearings.

"I am awfully sorry, miss," the porter said
apologetically, pushing back the contents of
the trunk.   "It was quite an accident.   I'll
tie a bit of rope round it."   He carried it into
the station and then turned round.   "Why,
the next train doesn't go for the next two hours
and a half, miss.   You'll have time to get it
mended.   There's a shop not two minutes off."

"Oh! it doesn't matter," she said; "it can
be mended at Bridgwater," and sat down in the

waiting-room. A half-frightened sense of adventure came over her. She had never been a journey alone in her life before, and the fact that she was going to take it without the knowledge of anyone who had control over her made the little one to Susan seem a daring thing to undertake. She felt as if a terrible penalty must await it, but the penalty would not come, at any rate, till the end of a week. She counted the days to Mr. Belcher's return. Six whole ones before he would drive up in a hansom to Montague Place with Dottel—poor ugly Dottel—on the seat growling and looking out at the people passing by. He would ask for her and hear that she had gone to Bridgwater without his leave, without telling him, without his money, for she had left the two pounds on the mantelpiece in the dining-room. She wondered if he would telegraph or write or come. "But I won't go back," she thought. "I will stay with Susan all my life or hide myself somewhere else." Then, stunned and dazed at the events of the morning, she fell half asleep, while some jibbering fiend whispered to her, " You'll have to go back—you'll have to go back—he'll make you, and then he'll treat you a thousand times worse. Some day he'll kill you."

" He won't," she answered in a dream, "for I will kill myself."

"You will never do that," the fiend said, "for you want to live ; and if he does not kill you, you'll have to live years—and years—and years." Then a voice in the distance, that was wholly different, and seemed to belong to some pitying soul that stretched out its arms to her and was sorry, tried to comfort her. "The world is very beautiful," it said ; "you wanted to walk all over it ; it is full of joy and sorrow and work to do, and somewhere in it someone has need of you, just as Mrs. Oswell said." The tears came into her eyes, and her throat was choked by a sob.

"I know, I know ; but I am stunned and blind and afraid," she answered. "What can I do ?—where shall I go ?—oh, take me and hide

me away from the life I have known, and let
me be happy—just a little bit happy and safe,
and hidden from him." She put her head
down her breast, in order to show no sign
while the people passed to and fro, each one
full of his or her own concerns. Then there
came back to her like a message out of the
past, with a little reproach in it for not having
understood it at the time, Mr. Oswell's talk at
Windermere about the boats to the Mediterranean, and the little places along the coast
that his wife had despised. She held her
breath as she thought of them. It seemed a
daring, desperate thing to do, but she was a
daring, desperate woman. "If I could get to
one of them," she said to herself, "he would
never find me." It would be far better than
going to Susan. She thought of the blue sea
and the mountains, and Mrs. Oswell's description of how the people ate macaroni and basked
in the sun, and went to mass in the morning,
and sat round their little oil-lamps in the evening. It all came back as if it had been but

yesterday. "He said that the boats started
from Southampton on Wednesdays. I will go
—I will go at once!" she cried, starting up;
but she did not know even how to get to Southampton, or from what station the train went,
and she was afraid to make many inquiries lest
Mr. Belcher should trace her, and drag her
back, gagged and pinioned. Chance befriend-
ed her: for once in her wanderings she had
passed a shipping office in Waterloo Place,
and it occurred to her that the best thing to
do would be to go there and inquire, even
though she missed the ship for this week. She
rescued her broken trunk from the heap of
luggage among which it had been placed, and,
breathless and almost irresponsible, drove off.

Four hours later she was at Southampton.
The boats sailed from there, surely enough,
though the day of sailing had been changed to
Thursday. She had decided that it was better
to fly from London at once, and taken her
passage to Genoa. She took it at the office in
Waterloo Place, and as Miss Katherine Kerr,

for when the clerk had asked what name he
was to put on her ticket, she did not dare to
give her husband's ; moreover, she never wanted to be known by it again.

The Windermere experience taught her how
to enter the hotel at Southampton, and desper-
ation kept up her courage. She arrived in the
afternoon, and like a woman in a dream walked
about the place, looking across to the Isle of
Wight, and staring at the tall masts of the
ships and the busy life along the shore. Everything was so strange to her, and like the set-
ting of a dream. She wondered if it were her
own self who walked about, or someone else
into whom she had been changed. As if some
impulse which was not her own controlled her,
she stopped before a trunk-shop and remembered her broken box. The shop was full of
leather cases, P. and O. boxes, such as people
usually take on board ship for their cabins.
She had seen the passengers at the station
arriving with them from other ships. So she
entered, and bought one and a Gladstone bag,

and then, trying to imagine what else she
needed to make her resemble an ordinary
traveller, became possessed of wraps and other
things that helped to disguise her if hereafter Mr. Belcher tried to trace her by description. All this was done by chance or
fate rather than intention of hers. The old
box was given to the chambermaid, who, seeing that Katherine was young and sad, for
some sympathetic reason told her that in a
week's time she was going to America to
keep house for a brother whose wife had
died.

In the night, that first night she had ever
been adrift in the world, with no one having
knowledge of her whereabouts, some sort of
reaction overtook her. The thing she was
doing seemed so unbelievable when she calmly
considered it. She was running away from
home, from everybody who knew her; she
was going out into the strange world alone,
among people she had never seen, and to some
place of which she did not even know the

name, and that was only a vague dream to her. She sat up in bed and looked out into the darkness, and considered her position in sheer astonishment. "Perhaps I ought to have gone to Uncle Robert," she thought. But she knew that, though he had given her two hundred pounds in case of an emergency, he would sternly disapprove of her conduct. "A woman must submit to the authority of her husband," he would have told her, and sent her back. Or Susan? Susan would send her back, too, cowed and submissive. She was quite right not to go to Bridgwater. She wished she had written to Mr. Belcher before leaving his house, and told him that he was free, that she would never trouble him again nor cost him anything, and that he might marry anyone else if he liked, for he should never see her again. It would have been a good thing to do. She ought to have thought of it in London, for presently she would not dare to write lest the postmarks betrayed her hiding-place. But it did not

10

matter.   He would only be glad that she
was gone, and go on with his life contentedly
enough.

"I will never go back," she said aloud.   It
was not as if she had made him happy, or as
if he had liked her or needed her.   She had
only been in his way.   If she had stayed with
him he would have broken her heart, or else
—and she looked up as if she were listening
to something; it was the recognition of a
strange possibility in her heart, and she could
hardly believe it—or else he would have roused
her and made her a bad and cruel woman, and
some day she might have killed him.   She
understood now how it was that dreadful
things were done.   Oh, it was terrible! she
thought.   No people in the world ought to
marry unless they felt that if no ceremony at
all had ever been known they would have
lived together just the same all their lives because they could not bear to live apart.   That
would be marriage, but they were not married
—he and she—and she would never say that

they were again. When she had arrived at this conclusion, she put her head down on the pillow once more and tried to sleep; but she dreamt that Mr. Belcher was sending down a shower of blows upon her, and awoke to realise with shuddering thankfulness that she was beyond their reach.

She went on board as early as possible the next day, and breathed freely as she went over the gangway. The stewardess told her that, as there were so few passengers, she could have a cabin to herself. The possibility of a companion had not occurred to her, but she recognised the danger she had escaped. She tried to stay on deck and watch the hurry and bustle of getting away, but it was no good —she could not bear it. She went to her cabin and shut the door and sat on the sofa berth beneath the port-hole, and looked at her new P. and O. box and the bag beside it, and trembled with exhaustion—the exhaustion of continual excitement, of fear and daring. There were voices and footsteps coming on board, and the loud click-clicking of the crane hoisting bales of goods on to the deck. Then the donkey-engine began, and presently the ropes were gathered in and the captain's stentorian voice gave orders from the bridge; it was like music to Katherine's ears. More going up and down and crowding and talking, the occasional rattle of a glass or dropping of some heavy load, a shriek from the funnel and the stoppage of the donkey-engine, a tremulous feeling that shook the boat, and the rushing of the water at the side.

"We have started," she cried, and rose to her feet, trembling with excitement again. She threw off her gloves and hat, and, kneeling upon the berth, looked out of the porthole. Yes, they had started. The shore was receding farther and farther from the ship. She looked at the widening sea with a strange, unbelieving joy. An indescribable sense of security came over her; a sob came into her throat. Suddenly her eye caught a gleam of gold ; it was the wedding-ring on her third finger. With a quick movement she drew it off and flung it into the water. "It is all over," she cried, "and I am free ! "

CHAPTER IX.

Four days—a long draught of freedom and contentment. The sea had been rough enough, but it was deepest blue now, and the sunshine was pricking it everywhere with gold. Light and warmth everywhere, while a happy breeze went by, touching the travellers on its way. Katherine's face had lost the hunted look it wore the day she came on board. The captain stared at her with undisguised admiration, and wondered what might be her history. Her fellow-passengers were disposed to be friendly. But there was a natural dignity that stood her in good stead, and helped her to keep them at a distance. "Sensible girl," a middle-aged man going out to Venice said to himself; "she knows her own business and

means to mind it." The ship arrived at Gibraltar on the fifth day, and the passengers
went ashore for a few hours. It was early
morning; the market was crowded, the main
street full of life. Katherine hesitated; she
was half afraid, but she remembered that she
was by herself, and hoped to be so forever,
and gathered courage. She walked a little
way towards Europa Point, then the courage
fled; she turned round quickly and went back.
"Not yet, not yet," she said to herself. "I
know it is all beautiful and strange, but I am
blind and deaf still, and feel safe nowhere but
on board." The ship was deserted; nearly
everyone was ashore. She sat on deck and
watched the Rock and its wonderful gardens,
which were a mass of bloom, and the people
moving to and fro, and she looked across at
the African coast on the other side and thought
how wonderful it was to see the edge of another quarter of the world. Mr. Belcher and
Montague Place seemed to have passed out of
her life, but the events of the last week had

left her tired. By and by she would feel better.

The day wore on, and the passengers began to return. "They will ask me questions if I stay here," she thought, and went down to her cabin again—that blessed little cabin in which she had sealed her freedom when she flung her wedding ring through the port-hole. It was as if she had drawn her pen across a terrible chapter in her life that had only by some dire chance been written on her memory. It was so good to lie on the sofa, with the port-hole open, to feel the sweet air coming in—air that Mr. Belcher had never breathed in his life—and all the sounds of happy life from the shore. She heard voices as of arrivals, and heavy luggage being carried on board—quantities of it. It was put down with a thud on the lower deck, ready for carrying below or into the cabins. There was a light footstep, and a woman's voice said merrily:

"What a clean little ship it is! We shall

enjoy our three days on board her," as it went past Katherine's cabin-door.

"As long as the Immortal doesn't mind it, I don't care," a man answered. "If he does mind it, and he's going to be next us, I do."

"Look after the Mummy, George darling, and I'll take care of the Immortal," the woman, whose voice seemed familiar to Katherine, answered back. Then she heard no more— only the sound of the donkey-engine beginning again, and more footsteps and voices and confusion and hurrying, and she knew that the ship was being made ready to move. She longed for it to go on. She had discovered that she loved the sea and board-ship ; it made her feel like an infant being rocked in a huge cradle by a wise and loving mother ; she would be sorry when they reached Genoa, but that was three days ahead—three good days of life to live. How beautiful it was to be alone ! "I should like to spend a lifetime in this dear ship at sea," she thought. Then she looked up though the port-hole again. The donkey-engine had stopped, the Rock was going backwards, the ship had started. She waited another hour in her cabin, then put on a shady hat and went on deck. There were only two or three people about, the middle-aged man was reading a novel, and the German husband and wife who had come on board at Southampton stood watching Gibraltar as the ship sped on away from it. Suddenly she came upon an old lady sitting by the wheel-house on a deck-chair; a shawl was wrapped round her shoulders, a railway-rug had been put carefully over her knees.

"This must be the Mummy," she thought. A closely written letter was pinned to the railway-rug, so that it might not blow away: its owner read it again and again while she knitted. She looked up as Katherine passed, and her ball of brown worsted rolled on to the ground. Katherine picked it up, and saw by chance that the letter pinned to the railway-rug was dated from Simla.

"Thank you," the old lady said. She was

not very old—sixty, perhaps—but she looked delicate and even feeble. She had grave dark eyes and a sallow complexion, and quantities of soft grey hair, half hidden in an old-fashioned white lace cap. But above all there was something stately about her. "What a beautiful face!" Katherine thought to herself, as she turned away. "I wish my mother had lived and looked like that, and had loved me." Two people came up the companion and passed by her; she did not see their faces, but they were evidently young. The man was tall and soldierly, the woman was graceful. They went to the old lady.

"Are you all right?" asked the man affectionately.

"I've arranged all your things in your cabin," said the woman, and again the voice sounded familiar, "the Immortal is happy, and so are we." Katherine walked the length of the ship and came back to meet the strangers face to face; with a little cry of surprise she recognised one of them and hesitated.

"Kathy!" The speaker was pretty and piquant: she held up her hands with delight and surprise. "My dear Thing! How did you arrive here? Don't you know me? I was Alice Irvine, and went to Mrs. Barrett's." A little dismay took hold of Katherine, though her face lighted up with pleasure. "I wondered what had become of you," her friend continued. "I should have gone to your castle, only I know that the Ogre didn't allow visitors."

"I thought you were in India," Katherine said, "and I am so glad to see you. You were the only friend I ever had except Mrs. Barrett," she added with unconscious pathos.

"We were in India, of course, but we went back just a year ago, so that the baby might be born in its native land—in English native land, you know. It's downstairs with the ayah. And this is George; his other name is Alford, and so is mine, but he's much nicer when you call him by his Christian name. I have been married four years."

" What a long time ! "

" Well, I was much older than you, dear. I see you are not married yet," and she looked down at Katherine's ringless finger. " Now speak to George, and shake hands—you two."

" I have often heard of you, Miss Kerr," he said, doing as he was told. " How was it you never wrote to us ? "

" Because I never wrote to her, she lived in a castle with an Ogre," his wife explained. " What has become of him, Kathy ? "

" He has gone to Australia to look after some grandchildren who have turned up."

" And left you alone ? "

" Yes," said Katherine faintly, wondering what she had better do. She could not explain on the spot that she was running away from her husband.

" I didn't go to Woolwich this time," Mrs. Alford went on ; " there was not a soul I knew left there, and I saw Mrs. Barrett's death in the paper, so I didn't go to Shooter's Hill."

" I wonder if she saw my marriage in the

paper," Katherine thought. "If she was in India she probably didn't. Where are you going?" she asked aloud.

"At present, my dear, we are going to Genoa, in order to take George's mother so far," and Alice nodded at the knitter.

"She looks such a sweet old lady."

"We came to England on her account as well as the coming baby's. She is a dear! But she is delicate, and can't get about much. When we had to go to Gibraltar, she went with us; and we had a lovely winter," she sighed in a voice of deep contentment. "Now we are suddenly sent back to India—Heaven knows why. I like it, of course, because my people are there; but George is sorry to leave his mother, though he has a brother at Lahore to console him. We are to pick up the P. and O. at Brindisi, and have left our heavy luggage to go by it from Gibraltar. Meanwhile, we have skipped on in advance in this little boat, in order to take the Mummy as far as Genoa, and stay a week with her there. She

is on her road to summer quarters—she wants
to stay abroad another six months."

"All alone?" said Katherine, as they sat
down on one of the side seats to continue their
talk. Travelling was not such a venturous
thing, after all, she thought, if a delicate old
lady could go about by herself.

"Yes, alas! That's the sad part of it. A
niece was going with her, but she broke down
at the last moment, married a man who looked
like a nigger, and went to China instead.
Some people have no morality," she added,
as her husband sauntered back to them. "I
think it makes them more amusing, but George
would be shocked if I said it before him. He's
a beautiful dear," she added, looking up at him
saucily, "but he is the properest person in the
world; so is his mother, so is Jim—the most
adorable Jim."

"Goose," said her husband. "What are
you talking about?"

"I don't know," she said; "I never do—
it's too much trouble. Oh! I was saying that

you and the Mummy and Jim are all three very strait-laced, and that a little crookedness would be rather amusing. But I only say it to shock you, dear," and she made a face at him, "and I don't know in the least how it came into this conversation."

"I think they are in love with each other," Katherine said to herself, with the odd sense of witnessing a new phase of human nature. For even the Oswells, always on easy, happy terms, did not look at each other as these two people did.

"And now," said Alice Alford, picking up the thread of her talk with difficulty, "the Mummy has got to manage her summer alone till she can persuade a stray relation to come out to her. That's why we are taking her as far as we can on our way, and left Gibraltar sooner than we should have done."

"Why don't you take her to India?"

"Her health won't stand it, poor darling! or she would like it. Her other boy is there.

She has only two children—George and Jim ; and she worships Jim, who has a civil appointment out in Lahore. She is miserable because he has been very ill;· but he is getting better, and gone to Simla. Simla is the place where all lively Indians under thirty go to when they die—if their ghosts don't care to come home— not that Jim is going to die, bless him. He is only twenty-seven, and as handsome as he is high, which is five foot ten. All the same, I prefer George myself. Now, Kathy, tell me, where are you going? I always called her Kathy," and she looked up at her husband again, "because there is something austere about Katherine—which doesn't suit her. Come, give an account of yourself. You have told me nothing yet."

"You haven't given her a chance," Mr. Alford laughed, and sauntered off so that he might not interfere with confidences. Then Katherine explained that she was going to Genoa, and that she did not know what she was going to do afterwards.

11

"You poor thing! Are you left loose on the world? And are you rich?"

"Yes, I am left loose on the world, and have all my fortune with me."

"Good heavens! Is it much? We'll rob you."

"It's a little more than two hundred and fifty pounds."

"Has the Ogre cast you adrift with that noble sum?"

"He hasn't cast me adrift," Katherine answered; "he'll give me more if I want it."

"And why have you left Shooter's Hill!" Mrs. Alford asked. "And why didn't you go to Australia with the Ogre?"

"The lease of the house ran out, and the Ogre did not want to take me to Australia."

"I see; so he gave you some money and left you to look after yourself. Well, I don't think it's proper for you to be roving about the world without a chaperon. But come and look at the 'Immortal!' it's the beautifulest Immortal that ever you did see."

"You seem so happy," Katherine said, much as she had once said to Mrs. Oswell.

"Happy?" her friend answered, with more gravity than she had displayed before. "I should think so! Why, I'm married to the dearest boy on earth, and have the sweetest baby, and a grey-haired angel for a mother-in-law, and all the other belongings are perfection. Heaven will be thrown away on me when I get to it. I have everything I want in this world," and she gave a sigh of content. "Don't you think George is very handsome?"

"Very," Katherine said, with a laugh in her blue eyes.

"He's just the sweetest, beautifulest old darling in the world," his wife remarked, with extreme satisfaction. "I think I know all about you, Kathy, dear," she went on. "The Ogre has deserted you; given you some money and left you to look after yourself. You can't be very happy, I'm afraid."

"Not very, perhaps," Katherine answered gently. "I feel like a waif. But it is a

beautiful world," she added, "and I like
going about looking at it.   I always feel
as if it were my own big estate—it is as
much mine as anyone else's—and I'm so proud
of it!"

"What a funny idea!" Mrs. Alford said.
"But you always had funny ideas.   Do you
remember the crane, and how you used to
think that Anne Boleyn danced with her head
in her pocket?"   And then they laughed and
went to see the Immortal.   It was a soft little
thing, with yellow hair and blinking blue
eyes.   Katherine stooped and kissed it, and
looked at it curiously.

"May I hold it for a moment?" she asked,
and took it in her arms, and felt afraid and
like a stranger in the world, unused to ordinary human experiences.   "What a wonderful
thing it must be to have a little child of one's
very own!" she said.   "Only I think one
ought to love—to love its father very
much."

"Why, of course," Alice said, staring

at her. "If you didn't, it would be horrible."

"She's awfully lovely, darling," George
Alford said to his wife that evening. "Her
face is like a lily on a long stalk, and there's
something fascinating about her. She ought
not to be going about by herself."

"She says she is a waif, and going to live
at some little Italian place."

"She and the mother had better join on."

Then Mrs. Alford clapped her hands.
"George," she said, "you are a wonder! You
always think brilliantly, even by chance.
Why shouldn't she and the mother really join
on? It would be a comfort. Let us stick to
Katherine and make the mother take a liking
to her. It will simplify matters beautifully."

Before they reached Genoa Katherine was
as intimate with the Alfords as though she
had seen them constantly all her life; but it
was they who did most of the talking, for she
was naturally reserved, and her position made

her more so, though in her heart she said
many things to them of which her lips were
silent. Had Alice not been married she would
have probably told her everything ; as it was,
that lady's chance remark about the Alfords'
love of propriety, for one thing, prevented it.
Besides, the life behind her was finished ; she
could no more speak of it than she could open
a grave and hold up the dead within. She did
not feel that she had committed a crime in
what she had done, but rather that she was
justified. Her marriage had been a mere
mockery of one with a man of whom she could
not think without a shudder. Thank God, she
had left him ! · She looked forward, and not
behind, feeling that with every hour that
passed she was journeying towards life and
love. and freedom : already she was tasting
their sweetness. She was almost happy—for
she chased away every disturbing memory—
for the first time in her life.

She delighted in the Alfords, in Alice's
ceaseless chatter and George's slow and in-

dulgent tones, in the little soft Immortal, and above all in the old lady. She had never known a beautiful old lady before. She liked to look at her face and watch her little stately manners that were so lovable, yet that would somehow make it impossible, Katherine felt it even then, to give her a difficult confidence. She liked to sit by her and watch her knit, and hear her talk of her other boy in India, the "adorable Jim," as Alice called him, and to wait upon her with those little services that a girl finds it so sweet to pay to one who is old and picturesque.

"I wish you would go with her somewhere, Kathy dear," Alice said; "she is all alone in Europe; don't you think you could join your plans to hers?"

"I should like it," Katherine answered. "She's so beautiful with her white hair and stately figure; but I can't think that she would care to have me with her."

"My dear, she has taken an enormous fancy to you," Alice answered decisively.

"But she knows so little of me."

"But I know so much, and I've told her everything about you. She says you look so good, and altogether has taken a violent fancy to you. Goodness goes a long way with her, she and George—oh! and with dear old Jim, too, out in Lahore."

"Alice, I can't——" she began, but George Alford appeared.

"George, she's rather refractory," Mrs. Alford said. "Come and tell her she must do as she's told, and that it is strictly improper of her to be going about the world alone."

"Miss Kerr," the old lady said that evening, "my children tell me that you will be content to join your plans with mine for the summer?"

"If you care to have me," Katherine answered meekly, feeling like an impostor, but resolutely putting the feeling from her. And so it was settled. They stayed at Genoa till the George Alfords went on to Brindisi to meet their P. and O.

Mrs. Alford turned to Katherine as her children disappeared. "My dear," she said, "I am glad they have left me you, for I feel that we shall love each other." The tears came into Katherine's eyes so that she could not speak, but the old lady saw her face and was satisfied.

CHAPTER X.

In the year that Katherine journeyed towards it, no horrible railway spoilt Generoso, it was merely a beautiful mountain in Italian Switzerland, with a good but simple hotel half an hour from the summit, and a farm and a few scattered dwellings for the peasants and goatherds. The hotel was whitewashed outside, the lizards ran over it in the sunshine. There was a little flight of stone steps leading up to the entrance, over which hung the great bell that clanged to announce an arrival. In front was a plateau that formed some sort of garden, and had a summer-house at either corner. But it is too well known, too well remembered as it was before the "improvements" came, to make description necessary. Kath-

(168)

erine and Mrs. Alford went up from Mendresio
after staying at the Italian lakes in late June.
It was a little early and chilly for a mountain-
place; but the old lady took a sitting-room
with a fireplace—the only one on that floor—
and when the clouds hung about and no sunshine came to lift them into heaven or to carry
them down to the valley, they sat and warmed
themselves by the crackling wood. Then it
was that they talked of India; of Alice and
her husband, who were at Bombay; and of the
Immortal, who was growing more beautiful
every hour, so the weekly letter told them;
and of Jim, who was slowly getting better. It
seemed to Katherine that though she had never
seen him that she knew Jim best of all, for his
mother loved him best, and never tired of talking about him.

There were but a few people at the hotel at
first, but as the days wore on more and more
arrived. Katherine used to watch for them,
and think how good it was to see them coming
up from the plains below, happy in their holi-

day time; or seeking health on the beautiful mountain-top, with hope written on their faces. For many invalids came round the winding pathway: overworked men and delicate women; and some who were like to die but did not know it.

It was mid-August. The world was full of summer and drowsy happiness: a deep blue sky was overhead. The hotel was nearly full; but Mrs. Alford and Katherine kept to themselves, and were wholly satisfied with each other.

"I do not want to talk to these strangers," the old lady said. "You never know who people are in hotels, nor what burden one may be taking on one's self with new acquaintance. I am very shy of making any."

"You trusted me——" Katherine began.

"But Alice had known you so long, my dear. And then I loved your face. I felt that you were good, and goodness is an old-fashioned virtue that appeals to me."

"I'm not good," she answered, "but I want to be, and I will be if I can."

"I remember once having a terrible lesson," Mrs. Alford went on. "It was when my dear sister and I were in San Remo some years ago —the year the boys first went to India—we made acquaintance with a Mrs. Simpson. Such a pretty woman, with a little boy of six to whom she was devoted. We thought she was a widow, but it turned out that she had run away from her husband——"

"Perhaps her husband had ill-treated her?"

"That would be no excuse, my dear. A woman must stay with him even if he ill-treats her, just as she must put up with her life even if it is full of pain. She has no business to run away from the one nor to dispose of the other."

"Suppose a girl were made to marry a man she disliked?"

"It isn't done in these days," the old lady said, shaking her head.

"But if she did marry him?"

"Then she must keep to it," the old lady
said. "It is part of a woman's duty to prove
that marriage is sacred and binding, and everything she does to weaken it she does to the dis-
advantage of her whole sex."

"But if the man doesn't love her?"

"She should try to win him, or bear her lot
in patience."

Then Katherine thought—"You must never
know; I must never tell you." And the desire
to do so passed out of her heart. "There are
many ways of looking at the same things, and
each may be a right one, but the person who
sees from one point cannot sometimes see from
another," she thought as she looked up to
watch the lizards running up the house in the
sunshine.

"Katherine, do you never get any letters?"
Mrs. Alford asked.

"No," Katherine answered, "my uncle is
in Australia. There is an old servant, but she
does not even know where I am." She gave a
long sigh, for she often wondered how Susan

was, and whether Mr. Belcher had sought her there.

"You must be very lonely, dear child?"

"I have been, but I like it," Katherine answered. "I like being with you, but I don't want to be with anyone else, and when you go back to England I shall stay somewhere alone and out of it."

"I hope one day you will marry," Mrs. Alford said tenderly. "Then perhaps you will be very happy."

"Oh, no!" Katherine answered shudderingly. "I know people are happy—I have seen them. Alice and George are. But marriage is a terrible thing: it is for one's whole life."

"Some day, if you love anyone very much," Mrs. Alford answered sadly, "you will think how short a time that is, and pray that it may be for a whole eternity too."

A still and sultry afternoon. Mrs. Alford was writing letters by herself. Katherine was

leaning out of her bed-room window—a narrow
slip of a room, looking towards the south and
the plains of Lombardy. From it she could
see two or three turnings of the pathway by
which the people came up from Mendresio.
They walked up in those days, or rode on
mules, or were carried in chairs by perspiring
porters; and the great bell rang when they
were seen on the last turn of the pathway before they reached the plateau. Katherine used
to look down from her window and watch them
come towards the little double flight of stone
steps before the door, while the landlord hurried out to welcome them and the mules were
unloaded. Once she thought how terrible it
would be to see anyone arrive who had known
her formerly, and for one moment the thought
paralysed her; then she remembered that Mr.
Belcher did not travel, and that Mr. and Mrs.
Oswell were certain to be in England, so she
put aside her fear and gave herself up to the
glorious summer and all it had brought her.
She was so happy, so full through and through

of sweet content. She was living the natural life of a girl who is with her mother : she was loved and cared for and spoken to with caressing words for the first time in her life ; she drank in joy every moment of her life and wished that she could live it over and over again.

She looked across to Lombardy, thinking that she ought to have made a sketch that morning for Mrs. Alford to enclose in a letter to India, and a little bit of white, low down in the distance, caught her eye. It was the white linen cap of a stranger who was coming up the pathway. He was twenty minutes off yet, and she knew that he would be out of sight again in a moment. She reached down the operaglass the Alfords had given her at Genoa and looked at him. He was on foot, but a mule carried his luggage, and the mule-driver lagged behind. She could tell that the stranger was a tall man. He wore tweed clothes, and a glass was slung across his shoulder. She did not see his face; he kept it turned towards the

12

plain till he was lost among the fir-trees, and she knew that a good ten minutes must pass before he emerged from them on the pathway higher up. And then she remembered the woman ill with consumption in the next room but one to hers, who had said by accident one day that she had left off having afternoon tea because it mounted up her bill. Katherine guessed that she was poor from the tone in which she said it, though she tried to make it disagreeable in order to disguise her poverty. Ever since at four o'clock she had made some tea, using Mrs. Alford's tea-basket, which she had borrowed, and some tea she had bought herself at Genoa after finding how bad can be the mixture that goes by the name of tea on board ship. She rang for the milk and lighted the spirit-lamp to boil the water. Then she thought of the stranger coming up the pathway, and went back to the window. He was just by the nearer turn. She watched him for full two minutes, and made out that he was young and good-looking.

" Five minutes more and he will be here," she said to herself, and went on with her tea-making. She carried a cup to Mrs. Alford at the end of the corridor, and poured out one for the consumptive woman, and as she did so there was the clang, clang, of the arrival bell. She went to the window and looked out. The stranger was crossing the plateau that had a summer-house at either corner. She turned away and knocked at the door of Miss Bennett's room.

"Come in !"

"I've brought you some tea."

"Oh ! thank you," the woman said sourly, "but I'm not sure that it agrees with me." She got up from the sofa on which she had been lying. "It's very good of you to take so much trouble," she said, as though she was half bored by it. But she took the tea in her thin hands and gulped it down eagerly.

"I will come for the cup in a few minutes," Katherine said, and hurried to her own room. Walking straight to the window she looked out. The stranger had just arrived. She looked down, trying to see his face, not expecting that he would see her. But, as though he had known that she was there, he raised his head, and they took a long look at each other. She knew him directly ; she had often seen his photograph. It was Jim Alford.

CHAPTER XI.

KATHERINE heard him come up the cocoa-nut-covered stairs and go along the corridor; someone was showing him the way. She listened to his footsteps, and imagined his face. He stopped at the end of the corridor, knocked, and called "Mother." Then she knew for a certainty that she was right.

Mrs. Alford opened the door quickly and fell into her son's arms. "Oh, my dear," she said, "this is a surprise."

"I thought you would say so," he laughed. "I told them not to tell you that I was coming, I wanted to drop down upon you unawares."

"My dear, oh, my dear, my dear!" she said again as she pulled him into the room and

(179)

pushed him gently into one of the velvet-
covered chairs with arms, beside the window,
"is it really you?"

"Yes—at least it seems like it."

"And are you better?" she asked, looking
at him as though she could hardly believe that
she was awake.

"Oh! I'm all right," he answered a little
uneasily, "though I have been pretty well rid-
dled with fever, I can tell you. However, it
has got me six months' leave, so I oughtn't to
grumble. Six months, Mummy! think of that
and sing a psalm. We can go to Jericho together if we like."

"We'll go to England, my son, and that
will be better. Tell me about your illness, and
how you managed the journey."

"Not much to tell," he said cheerily. "I
fell sick and was like to die; managed with
some diplomacy and a good many certificates
to get leave. Went by easy stages to Bombay,
took ship and sailed to Brindisi, crawled along
here. That's all. George and Alice send their

love ; the baby's a bouncer, and more beautiful than ever, so they'll tell you. Spent a day
with them all in Bombay. What have you
done with the pretty girl they found for you—
is she here still? Alice's friend, I mean."

"Yes, she's here,—and will be so glad to
see you, my dear."

"Oh! will she? That's your idea, Mummy.
If she's the one who put her head out of win-
dow as I arrived, I shall be glad to see her.
How long is she going to stay with you ?"

"Till I go back to England in September,
unless you want me, dear boy, to go anywhere
with you. She's so good and unselfish, that
I'm sure she would give me up."

"That's all right, then. Now let us talk
about somebody else. I was so sorry about
your illness last winter, nearly came home,
with or without leave." He took his mother's
hands and kissed them. "Still it was a comfort to you, wasn't it, having George and Alice
and the baby? By Jove! what a fuss people
make about a baby when they have one for the

first time. It is such a pity they don't begin
with twins; upon my word I think it would
keep them quieter. What is your pretty girl
called—Kathy something, isn't it?"

"Katherine Kerr," the old lady said va-
cantly, too much overjoyed to do more than
look at him. "You must come and see her.
Oh, wait, I'll call her."

"No hurry, Mummy dear," he said, holding her back affectionately. "It's good
enough to see you."

She looked at him long and fondly. "You
are handsomer than ever," she said; "but
you don't look well."

"I shall soon," he answered. "I believe
you are more beautiful than ever, Mummy,
since we are paying compliments. What sort
of people are staying here?"

"I haven't looked at them. You see, I
have Katherine."

"I shall call her Kathy."

"You must call her Miss Kerr."

"All right, Mummy, I'll mind my man-

ners. Look here, I must go and do some unpacking, and then we'll have a long talk if you
like. I forget what number the beggar said
my room was, but it's a floor lower down, and
I daresay I shall find it."

"I'll come with you to the end of the
corridor, and we will knock at Katherine's
room. I want her to know how happy I am,"
she said lovingly.

Katherine heard their footsteps stop by
her door, and, opening it, stood facing
them.

"I watched you coming up," she said.
"I'm glad you are here. Mrs. Alford has been
so anxious about you." She looked at Jim
with clear blue eyes that were tender enough
when they turned to his mother—it proved
their capacity, he thought.

"I saw you leaning out of the window,"
he said merrily, "and guessed it was you.
Alice was always talking of you, and George
joined in the chorus."

"And the Immortal?"

"Only cried. No doubt he'll do better by and by. I hope you like this place, Miss Kerr; it is very kind of you to take care of the Mummy. She wants someone to look after her." He put his arm round Mrs. Alford's shoulder as they walked away.

"You must take him some walks, my dear," the old lady said, looking back. "She has had to go alone, poor thing," she continued to her son as they went down stairs. "For I am not able to do much; I was never a good walker, you know."

"You weren't bad, not what we call a strider, but——" Then their voices were lost in the distance. Katherine went back to her room, and, sitting down with her arms folded, looked out into space.

"He's very handsome," she said to herself. "He's much better looking than George; and how fond he is of his mother! It is lovely to see them together." Then just because her heart was light and hungered to take a little brightness somewhere, she went in to see the consumptive woman again, and asked if she could do anything for her.

"Would you like me to read aloud?—I often read to Mrs. Alford. Perhaps it would help you to go to sleep sometimes," she said humbly.

"No, thank you. I never heard any reading yet that satisfied me," said Miss Bennett ungraciously.

"I can understand that," Katherine answered. "I read some Browning to myself a little while ago, but could not imagine a living voice that would do him justice."

"I don't like Browning. You can take that volume of him away, if you like," Miss Bennett said, nodding to a book on the table. "I don't want it. I found it in a railway carriage."

"You don't want it?"

"I am not well enough for him. He did not write for sick and tired people. Besides, I dislike poetry. Prose is good enough for anything worth saying."

"Oh! don't say that," Katherine answered.

"Between poetry and prose there is the same difference that there is between speaking and singing."

"And speaking is better than singing," said the woman, "unless it is better than any that I ever heard. Poetry is never good enough, and singing is never good enough. Nothing is good enough in the world. That is what I have found," she added, with a long, weary sigh; "but I started expecting too much, and nothing has satisfied me."

"I expected nothing," Katherine answered, "and started knowing of nothing to expect, but now everything seems to be growing more and more beautiful as I journey on; but is there nothing I can do for you, Miss Bennett?"

"Only take away the Browning, and those flowers. Mrs. Ball, the woman with the thin husband, brought them. I dislike flowers near me; it disturbs me to see them die."

"I never thought of that," said Katherine gently; "I'll arrange them in my room and you shall come and see them only while they are fresh. It's too late for you to go to the Bella Vista to-night, I know, but I'll come and see if you are able to walk there in the morning. Good-bye, if we don't meet again—we sit so far apart at dinner, and you have so many friends at table that I never come near you down stairs."

"Not friends," said Miss Bennett, as Katherine was going out of the door, "and they are only kind to me because"—she waited till the door was shut—"they think I'm going to die."

Katherine went along the corridor to Mrs. Alford, for she knew that Jim was still down stairs. The old lady was standing up tall and stately, as she always looked when she rose to her feet.

"Just one moment to tell you how glad I am," the girl said gently, and held out her hands. "It was a beautiful surprise for you, and I don't wonder that you love him so much."

"My dear, there is no one like him in the world—like him and my other boy ; but Jim is my youngest and has always loved me most, and I am so proud of him." Her voice was low and full of happiness. She took Katherine in her arms, and kissed her as if from thankfulness to the day for its portion of joy. "He's the strongest man I ever knew, and as tender as a woman."

"I could hear it in his voice," Katherine answered, "and I am so glad for you—hush! he is coming. I will go away till dinner-time." She hurried softly along the corridor again, passing Jim on her way. "Your mother is waiting for you," she said, and turned a radiant face to him. "You will have two hours together before the dinner-bell rings," and she passed on. "What a world it is!" she thought, as she entered her room again; "the human beings in it are so wonderful: they fill one's heart." She sat down with an unaccountable happiness possessing her to think of the blessed lines on which her lot had fallen.

The watch on the table beside her—it was the one that Uncle Robert had given her—

pointed a quarter to six before she rose from her reverie. "Dear Uncle Robert," she said, as she noticed the time, "I wonder if you have found your children. I wish I had been a better companion to you all those years, but I was so afraid of you, for pain and trouble had made you stern. Perhaps some day I shall dare to go to you." She brushed out her hair; it was long and dark, with a little natural curl in it that made it fall softly on her forehead; she twisted it up into a large knot behind, as the Greek women twisted theirs in centuries gone by, and fastened into her waistband a little bunch of the flowers Miss Bennett had despised. Then she went back to the sick woman. "Let me take you down," she said, "Mrs. Alford has her son," and she drew Miss Bennett's arm through hers.

"You can't like being troubled with so helpless a creature," she grumbled.

"I am sorry—so sorry for you, but I am glad to be near you, because I am strong, and one's strength is like one's money," she laughed; "to be handed on—there's such a joy in spending it." She took Miss Bennett to her place at the far end of the table, then went to her own by Mrs. Alford. Jim entered five minutes later and sat down on the other side of the old lady. She was conscious of him every moment; it was like an intoxication. She heard his voice each time he spoke, and knew when he looked her way. To think that he was going to stay there with them, every day, perhaps for weeks to come, seemed the strangest thing on earth.

They went out of doors after dinner. Katherine tried to leave the mother and son together, but he came swiftly up to her as she was taking a side path towards the farm.

"My mother thinks that if I ask you very humbly you will, perhaps, take me to the Bella Vista," he said.

"I will take you without the humility," she answered; "but would you not like to stay with her this first evening?"

"She says it will only take us twenty minutes to get there and back, and then we can drink our coffee with her."

"Then let us start," and they walked on together.

"She's the handsomest girl I've seen these five years," Jim Alford said to himself. "Wonderful expression her face has—both brightness and sorrow in it."

"How long are you going to stay?" she asked.

"I have six months' leave. My mother talks of remaining here for a bit; then we shall go to England. When are you going home?"

"I have no home," she answered with a strange little smile, as though the knowledge pleased her.

"I know," he answered; "Alice told me. Your belongings consist of an ogre in the shape of an uncle—the description is hers, of course, not mine—who went to Australia."

"He isn't an ogre, though he did go to Australia, and I am fond of him."

"Beg pardon," he laughed. "I daresay

13

he's awfully nice, and personally I'm rather inclined to ogres, though he isn't one, you say.
Are you going to stay abroad all the winter?"

"Yes, all the winter."

"Where?"

"I don't know yet; I never look forward."

"Better not," he said with a gravity that
surprised her. "If the present is worth anything it's better to live in it. You'll think me
an awful duffer, but I want to sit down on that
seat there, if you wouldn't mind. I have not
been through with my fever very long, and
that pull up to-day was rather a long one."
His face was pale, he was trembling with cold.
"It's nothing," he said presently, with a shudder; "the plaguy thing comes back to torment
one now and then."

"You have been very ill, I know," she said
anxiously.

"Ill! Nobody knew how bad I was. I
was afraid they would tell the poor Mummy.
As a matter of fact, I bothered about getting
the leave because I thought I should never see

her again. But the voyage did wonders for me, and I daresay this place will set me up, and the Mummy and——" he was going to say "you," but he stopped, and said "all of it." He looked up at her gratefully. "It was such a comfort to know that you were with her."

"How did you know? You've only seen me to-day."

"I know everything about you," he answered. "All about Shooter's Hill, and the crane, and his one leg, and Eltham Palace. There, you see, I'm quite set up in your history."

"And I know something about yours, but not much," she answered; "you live at Lahore and——"

"That's enough: there isn't any more, except that I have a house there and live in it all by myself."

"You ought to get married," she said simply.

"Never saw anybody yet I wanted to

spend all my life with. Did you? I believe I could go a little bit farther, if you like."

"Let me give you an arm," she said without a bit of coquetry.

"There's something awfully straight about this girl," he thought, "and she's perfectly beautiful to look at.—"Thank you," he said; "I will, if I can't get along. I'm all right at present. Did you?"

"Did I—what?"

"Ever see anyone you wanted to spend all your life with?"

"No, never," she answered fervently, "never, but I think," she added, "that people are very good and kind. I have felt that more than anything else lately," she added, as if she spoke from conviction rather than experience.

"Yes, I'm sure they are—uncommonly good lot, on the whole—a few exceptions, of course."

"Oh, yes; there are exceptions," and she shuddered.

"Beastly shame," he thought: "someone

has helped her to find that out already. I should like to know who it was. I'd make things a bit uneasy for him or her. Hullo!— here we are!" he exclaimed, as they came upon the view at Bella Vista. "By George, it is splendid! I'd no idea that it was so fine." They stood together, looking in silence on the magnificence that had suddenly burst upon them.

"It makes one thankful for life, with eyes to see and ears to hear," she said; "to look at it even once is compensation for years—that— that—have been different."

"You speak as if you had suffered a great deal."

"Oh, yes, I have suffered," she answered, with a scared look in her eyes that came and went in a moment.

"I expect we all get our share. It's a good thing, I suppose. We none of us know any- thing till then, or understand it, at any rate."

"That is the pity of it, but don't let us talk of anything but happiness," she said, looking up with a smile. "I have tried so hard lately to drive—the rest out of my thoughts: and this is such a beautiful day for your mother, we ought to help her celebrate it. Come, let us go back, the coffee will be ready."

"I wonder if we could ever get down to that lake," he said, taking a last look at the view; "I mean to Lugano."

"There is a little path down," she said. "Not the one you came up by to-day, but a lovelier one. I went half-way down it the other afternoon while your mother slept."

"Let's try it one day," he answered, as if they were old friends, and it was a matter of course that they should explore together. "I say, are there any books here, at the hotel?"

"There are some novels in the library," she said, as they took their way back, "and I have got a stray volume of Browning Lyrics."

"We'll bring it out next time we come this way; it will fit in with the surroundings pretty well. But it's a dangerous book for two people to read together."

" Dangerous ? "

" Very," and he thought how blue her eyes were.

" You look tired, my son," Mrs. Alford said as they entered the summer-house.

" Yes, Mummy," he answered ; " even the happiest day one has known for years wears one out a little. I shall be stronger in a month or two, especially if I'm taken walks," and he looked at Katherine.

" I shall take you one every day," she said with a little smile, and left them together.

" At the end of a string," he said. " That's a wonderful girl, mother. There is so much in her face ; but I believe she has been ill-used at some time or other. However, she seems to be sunning herself in the time here."

"She never says so, but I fancy that her uncle must have ill-treated her."

" Old ruffian ! I daresay he did."

They went to Bella Vista again the next night, and up to the summit of Generoso two mornings later to see the sunrise.

"It is such a comfort to me that you are here, my dear," Mrs. Alford said to Katherine, "for I cannot walk, and but for you, there would have been no one to take Jim about."

"And he's not to be trusted alone, I suppose?" he laughed.

"No," said Katherine, "neither am I; that is why we are sent together."

The rest was only natural: in a week they were greatest friends, in a month—the happiest month of Katherine's whole life—they set their lives entirely by the wishes of each other. He was not strong, but he had wonderful spirits. "Not strong, but obstinate, describes me," he said one day. "You see, it is difficult to believe that up here Nature could do one a bad turn, and I never feel content till I have walked over every mile possible within reach of headquarters." And Katherine, who loved the world—just the beautiful world itself—before all things, or had till lately, usually went with him, while the old lady looked after them and rejoiced. She wanted her boy to marry—

she dreaded his going out to Lahore again, alone. "A wife would take care of him," she thought, and she had seen no one she liked so well as Katherine. Her reserve, her belief in the world, her absolute contentment in being cared for, her delight in simple pleasures, and a certain courtesy of manner that distinguished her, all appealed to the old lady, who considered the girls of the present day undignified or frivolous.

They went down to Lugano on foot one morning, and searched among the covered streets for curios, and lunched at the hotel, and took the train back to Mendresio, and rode up on mules to Generoso in time for dinner— a whole day to themselves—while Mrs. Alford stayed at home well satisfied to think of them together, or tried to devise means by which she might keep Katherine with her if she and Jim did not fall in love with each other.

"I wish you would come to England with us, my dear," she said one afternoon; "there is room for you at the little house at Chilworth, and I shall be all alone when he goes back to India in January.   Couldn't you come with me?"   Katherine was putting on her hat, and Mrs. Alford could not see her eyes, but there was terror in her voice as she answered—

"I can't go to England, dear Mummy; keep me till the last moment before you go, and then I will take my separate way."

"You are so young to be alone."

"I know, but it has to be."   She turned and faced her.   "I read a story book once," she said suddenly; "in it was a description of how lives were given out for people to live. They were done up in packets and all mixed up by the hand of Fate.   As the people were born one by one into the world Fate handed them a packet, and in it was the life they had to live.   They never knew what was going to happen to them except in that first moment which they could not remember.   But each one's life for good or ill was in his heart, and he had to live it.   You are going home with your son, dear Mummy, and I am going on."

"Where?"

"I don't know yet; but I shall soon."

"My child, it may be that you are to come to England, though you do not know it."

"Oh, no," and she turned away again.

"Katherine," the old lady said, trying to see what lay behind the troubled blue eyes, "I do not know what your life was there, but I think you were very unhappy."

"Yes," and she nodded her head, "I was very unhappy. I never had any happiness at all, save that which the beauty of the world gave me, till I left England, and saw you that day on board ship. Here is Jim"—for they had soon learnt to call each other by Christian names. "You see, you and Alice were school-fellows," Jim had explained, "and that is one reason why we should not treat each other with any respect; and then we are not in London, and we both like the Mummy, and lastly it's such a bore to be Miss Kerr-ing and Mr. Alford-ing each other, and we never do it behind each other's backs." Her face lighted up as he entered, and with a sigh of relief she chased away her memories.

"You and Mummy appeared to be having an argument when I entered," he said, as they went on their way to the farm. "What was it about?"

"We were talking of the end of September."

"Leave the future alone," he answered. "I believe in taking the portion dealt out for the day and getting all the good one can out of it."

"Sometimes one is forced to think about it against one's will," she said in a low voice.

He looked at her for a moment before he answered. She wore a white dress and a big white hat. She looked tall and slim and very young; but there was a womanly sedateness about her that was very restful. He could imagine her living a simple country life, busy with domestic affairs, and finding intellectual employment enough for herself when they were done. "She would look uncommonly well," he thought, "at the head of a table, or riding. By Jove! how she would like the early morning Indian rides—awfully proud a man would be of her, too." He thought of his house in Lahore and the stillness that filled it now, and the courage it would take to break in upon it alone.

"That is true, I have thought of it a great deal lately, though as a rule I try to avoid it. I like my work," he added, "in India and Lahore. I have had such good days there. If the Mummy keeps well and fever deserts me, I should like the future to be like the past— plus one. And you?"

"I want it to be quite different from my past," she said quickly. "It will be. I am going on to places I have never seen and to people I do not know.

"But have you left no people you care for behind?"

"There's Uncle Robert, but he is in Australia; and Susan, she has her own people; and Mrs. Oswell, she has her husband. There are no others—no others in the world except the Mummy and you, and Alice and her husband, and the Immortal."

"Couldn't you pull me out of that little crowd and give me a place to myself?"

"It might be a bad place."

"Anything is better than a crowd. But, I say, do you mean always to be by yourself? You know, some day you might want to get married."

"Oh, no; never, never!"

"Well, that's encouraging," he thought, and they went on for a few minutes in silence. The pathway to the farm was defined by a primitive railing, only wide enough for one person to walk along it, yet somehow they managed to walk two abreast. They sat on three-legged stools at the farm, and drank milk out of little bowls, while the bottle that Katherine had carried in a straw basket on her arm was filled for the benefit of Mrs. Alford and Miss Bennett, who considered that tea-making was the event of the afternoon.

"We must come here on Sunday," Jim said as they went back. "The goatherds and the milkmaids dance in the evening. We will come and look on; it will be another memory."

"Yes."

He drew her hand through his arm. A sudden remembrance of Mr. Belcher made her shudder.

"This pathway is constructed for people to walk so," he said. "It is better than going separately, especially when you don't want to talk; and we are not in a very chattering humour this afternoon."

"Sometimes one lives more keenly in silence."

"What are you thinking of, Kathy?"

"I was thinking," she said, "that, even if it means pain and bitterness, or being very lonely, we should still be very thankful for our turn of human life. It would have been much worse to be a stone or a star instead of a human being."

" You are a queer girl," he answered.   " I wonder if you know——"

She drew away the hand he had taken. "I don't know anything," she said, " and here we are back again."

CHAPTER XII.

SEPTEMBER was creeping into the autumn. The darkness gathered more and more into the nights, and the days were growing chilly.

"What a happy summer it has been!" Katherine said to herself with a long sigh as she watched the sunset. "If it would only never come to an end! I wonder if the Mummy dreams how happy she has made me." But it was of Jim she thought. The whole world had changed since he came, and a sense of quick life that sometimes made her stand still for joy was in her heart. He and she remembered so much now—books they had read and sketches they had made, long saunterings in the sunshine and the twilight, and talks of

14   (207)

many things in which each listened eagerly to hear the other's view concerning them.

But the summer was nearly over.

"We ought to be getting to the plains," Jim said to his mother one night while they sat over the wood fire. Katherine was not with them then. It had seemed lately as if she preferred to spend her evenings alone. He looked at the clock once or twice, and towards the door as a footstep came along the corridor; but he turned away when it passed on. "I wonder what Kathy is doing?" he said at last.

"I think she likes to go and see Miss Bennett."

"I daresay; it appears to me that there's very little goodness of which she isn't capable. I've been studying her all these weeks, Mummy, and have come to the conclusion that she is a very remarkable person."

"I shall be sorry to go home without her."

"Take her with you."

"She won't go, my son; I have often asked her."

"I expect the Ogre bullied her. Mother, should you be glad if she cared for me?"

"Do you mean if she would marry you, Jim?"

"Yes, I mean that. I don't believe she would; for, though she seems to like being with me, she has never given me a word of encouragement all the time. I have grown fond of her," he said in a low voice, and stooped to kiss his mother. "I never cared for any other woman in my life, and I don't feel as if I could face going back to Lahore without her."

Just for one moment the old lady sat silent. Had not her son loved her best all his life? Even though she had wished it, a little dismay came into her heart when she realised that someone else had taken possession of him, but she swept it away.

"I'm very glad," she answered lovingly. "She is the sweetest girl I have ever met. I have often compared her with the underbred and over-educated young women we are always meeting nowadays."

"That's rather severe," he laughed. "But you are a dear mother. I say, if she won't go to England, couldn't we go on somewhere else and take her with us? Not to an hotel, for I always feel like a tame cat after a week in one; or else the women who sit and purr to each other, and the men who play draughts in the evening, make me feel pleasantly murderous. Let us take a villa to ourselves somewhere, with a garden for you to walk in, and not on the top of a confounded mountain—I beg your pardon, Mummy, but, you see, I can't do any climbing now—some place where we could drive about a bit, or perhaps she and I could ride."

"You had better speak to her first."

"Not too soon," he said, shaking his head; "she's been a little hold-offish lately, I'm afraid to rush it."

"Shall I try and find out?"

"No, a man likes to try his own luck. We are going out in the morning to make a sketch from the top—to present to Miss Bennett. She said she hated photographs. Perhaps something will come of it ; but don't ask me. I will tell you when there is anything to tell."

The door opened and Katherine walked in. " May I come ? " she asked. " They are playing Consequences downstairs, and I am tired. There's a new novel left behind by the young men who came up yesterday and wènt down to-day, and here it is : I stole it for the Mummy."

"I like to hear you call me that, dear," Mrs. Alford said, looking up with a smile. The colour came to Katherine's face, but she went on as though she had not heard.

"Miss Bennett is very angry because she was asked to write her confession in somebody's book, and she put down that her idea of happiness was silence, and the very young man—who is, I think, a student—said that he didn't believe it."

"Miss Bennett was having a row with the landlord this morning," Jim said. "I heard him remark as I entered the bureau, 'Unless that is done, Mademoiselle, we will consider that you leave on Saturday.'"

"Perhaps it is because she has not paid her bill. I am certain she is poor, and she is going to die," Katherine said, dismayed. "I don't mean yet—I mean that she will never get well. She is in a consumption; the doctor downstairs told me that. He said she was hanging on to life in the strange manner that people do sometimes, long after its joy had ceased. And she is poor: she betrays it in her face and her shrinking tones, and the things she denies herself. It seems as if death and poverty were trying which could gain upon her first."

"Couldn't we get some money to her? It must be an awful thing to be dying and stranded."

"Oh, I wish we could! But she is sensitive. It would be so difficult to manage."

"Oh—well, we will see. Are we going to

do our sketch in the morning?" he asked after a moment's silence.

"Shall we?" and she looked at Mrs. Alford.

"Yes, my love," the old lady said, and took the girl's hands and drew her face down and kissed it, and whispered, "I want you to go with him."

Katherine drew back abruptly. "Alice and I used to go out sketching long ago at Shooter's Hill," she said.

"As if you were sisters," the old lady said eagerly.

"Then Jim would be my brother."

"Oh, no; sister to Alice would make me your brother-in-law, which is better. Sisters bully their brothers, you know," he added quickly. "I say, did you put down your confessions?" he asked, merely for the sake of saying something. "I wonder what your idea of happiness would be?"

"Freedom. It is the most blessed of all things."

"There is a good deal of nonsense talked
about it," he said shortly; "it depends upon
what you mean by freedom.   Explain, mademoiselle."

"I can't," she answered.   "I am tired, and
must go.   Good-night," and with a kiss to the
old lady and a look to him, she went slowly
from the room.

He looked after her for a moment.   "You
women are strange beings, Mummy dear," he
said in a puzzled tone.   "But it is getting late,
let us separate also.   I have some letters to
write, and the post goes early."

.   "Good-night, my son."

"Now, then," he said when he was alone,
"let us see what can be done for Miss Bennett."   He looked up between the lines of his
letter of instruction to England to think about
Katherine.   "I can't make her out," he said
once or twice; "she is not a bit of a flirt, and
if I'm not an ass, she has sometimes looked as
if she cared about me; but she has a manner
that makes her absolutely unapproachable.

There's a curious mixture of simplicity and dignity about her that I expect takes a more experienced hand than mine to manage."

But Katherine, standing before the open window in her room, was quite content. "I am so happy," she said to herself, "so perfectly happy—only I want it never to come to an end. That is impossible," she sighed; "so I must be thankful to have known him and loved him, for I do love him with all my heart. I don't care what it costs me, or what I have to suffer for it by and by. If the pain is mine, so is the love, and so will be the remembrance. It can never make any difference to him; he will never know, and his mother will never know. Oh, it can't be wrong," she cried, "he shall never, never know—it can't be wrong!" She stopped before the volume of Browning, and, opening it at random, read as if in answer to her thoughts—

Let us be unashamed of soul,
  As earth lies bare to Heaven above !
How is it under our control,
  To love or not to love ?

"I wonder if he cares for me at all; but that doesn't matter, it can make no difference. I have to go my way and he to go his, and nothing could make any difference." A flood of memories overwhelmed her. "Oh, how could Uncle Robert do it—how could he be so cruel! For I did not understand—but after all, it was but the way that led to this, and to think that makes me even thankful for all I went through at Montague Place. I'm glad —glad—glad," she added, with a long sigh. "Jim has no need of me, that is one comfort; he will forget me as soon as I go, and while she has him his mother does not need me. It is only Miss Bennett who needs me, if anyone does." She put out the light and went to the window again; she wanted, with her great happiness, to look out at the world and up at the sky and into space, and not to keep it in a narrow room. "Why do people die for love, and why are they so miserable about it, I wonder? To know a man like Jim, and to love him, is surely enough to live for and be thankful. I shall be better all my life because of these days, no matter what comes after them. There is midnight as well as noon, and we must take both in our twenty-four hours. It seems such folly to grieve in the night, when one might lie still and think of the day and the happiness it brought one. That is what I shall do when I live alone in my little Italian place. I shall think of him and try to do all the good I can, if I am capable of any, just as a thank-offering for these dear days in which I have been so happy."

There was no going out the next morning. It was windy and rainy ; a thunderstorm was coming over from Italy, and the firs were wrapped in a heavy mist. "We must do our sketch another day," Katherine thought, looking disconsolately from the window on the staircase. The landlord's daughter came out of Miss Bennett's room ; she hesitated and stopped.

"Miss Kerr," she said, "can I speak to you ? " and she opened the door of an empty room. "I ought not to tell you, but I know you are a friend of Miss Bennett's, and perhaps you will not tell anyone that I have spoken to you. She has not paid us for some time ; it is not much, for she looked so ill when she came, that my father was sorry and said as little as he could, but she has not paid anything for weeks. I think my father would forgive her altogether, for he feels that she is poor, and he is sorry for her ; but she is so haughty, so bitter, and to-day she treated him with such scorn that he has declared she shall not stay any longer. I thought I would speak to her myself without his knowledge, but she is unbearable, and told me to leave the room."

" Let me pay her bill."

" Oh, no ! certainly not ; but if you could say something to her and make her a little more polite."

"It is very difficult. I will try, but I would not hurt her for the world. Be good to her—I know you will. She is going to die," Katherine said gently. She heard Miss Bennett coughing uneasily as she passed her door, and went in as if to soothe her. "I am so sorry," she said ; " the rain and mist are bad for you."

" It doesn't matter. I am tired of waiting first for one thing and then for another. Now it is for the sunshine." Her face was very weary.

" You will be better when it comes," Katherine said, and stroked the thin, badly shaped hands.

" I don't want to be better. I shall be glad enough to die. Life is too difficult to manage."

" It is very difficult," Katherine answered. " I think that we ought to share things more than we do. If the people who have happiness, for instance, would set about giving some to the people who have none ; if the people who were strong could take those who are weak to places where they would get well ; if every strong man carried a weak woman—— Oh ! I am talking nonsense."

" I have nothing to share," Miss Bennett said grimly.

"I have been thinking of something that you could do for me," Katherine said, a happy thought striking her, "and it has come out of this philosophy. I am all by myself in the world, and I am very strong and happy, and have money. I want you to share all my things, my happiness and strength and loneliness. I have no one to take care of; if you would, let me take care of you. I would take you away to a little warm place in Italy, and you should get strong again. I should like to begin at once," she added, "though we needn't go away from here directly."

Miss Bennett looked up quickly. "I suppose they have told you that my bill is not paid—or you heard me speaking about it in the bureau yesterday. It is not convenient to me to pay it just now."

"Let me pay it. I have plenty; and if by and by you have plenty and I have none you can do the same for me. That is what I am trying to propose—that we share things, you and I, for we are both alone in the world."

"I don't want it, thank you," Miss Bennett answered, in her usual ungracious manner. "I have written to England. They can wait for their bill; I don't care if it isn't paid at all. They make enough by the English; let them lose a little."

"Oh, but that would be so unpleasant for you!"

"Well," Miss Bennett said, looking up, "what then? I don't want to take a friendly leave of the world. I should be sorry to go if I found it too pleasant. It is better to feel a satisfaction in dying than a regret."

"In dying?" Katherine said sadly.

"I know what is before me well enough." She took her left hand away from Katherine and stroked it with the right one, looking curiously the while at its transparency. "I know what is before me. What does it matter? I have lived, and am going to die. Why do people make so much fuss about it? Life is a great deal of trouble."

"I wonder why you are so bitter."

"Things went badly with me when I was young, and I have never forgiven the people who made them so."

"Don't you think you might now?" Katherine pleaded.

Miss Bennett shook her head. "I was never able to forgive. Only God can do that, and even He needs reparation. I don't understand forgiveness among people who live a little while and then die. No forgiveness will undo a thing that is done, or unbury the years that were ruined. My youth was ruined by harshness and selfishness. It was done to make me suffer, I suppose. I want to make others worse for it sometimes. I feel as if I had a grudge against the world and everyone who lives in it. I can't help it. You mustn't think I'm not grateful to you."

Katherine stooped and kissed her, and felt that now she understood love's use and its divinity.

CHAPTER XIII.

SOME news came for the Alfords that obliged them to give up any idea of a villa abroad, so they arranged to stay at Generoso till the end of September, by which time, indeed, seeing that neither of them was strong, it would be necessary to descend, even though the hotel remained open. They meant to stay a week in Milan, at the Cavour, and then journey home. Jim reconciled himself by thinking that the bracing air of England, would do him good and fit him for a long spell of service at Lahore.

"Are you going to live there all your life?" Katherine asked.

"I expect so," he answered; "till I am sixty, at any rate, and pensioned off like a respectable old buffer."

15   (223)

"And when are you going back?"

"In January. Meanwhile there is the Mummy's house at Chilworth to see. She built it for herself while I was away."

"A red brick house standing alone," Mrs. Alford said, "near a wood. I wish you could come and stay there." But Katherine shook her head ruefully, for she felt this summer holiday was indeed coming to an end—less than another fortnight and it would be over.

Another fortnight! · And then she would never see him again. She had to go on into the world alone for the rest of her days. "But I don't care yet," she said to herself; "while there is another fortnight, how can I trouble about what is to come after?" So youth and its temperament conquered, and as the clouds lifted from the mountain the fear at her heart lifted too, and as the sun came out it brought her promises and intoxicated her with happiness and love. To look out across Italy or down at the firs, to watch for the morning postman, his leather bag slung across his shoulder as he appeared on the little turnings of the upward path visible from her window, to see the strangers coming and going, and all the time to feel her heart brim over with life: what joy it was—how could she think about the future?

A glorious morning at last, still and warm. Katherine and Jim Alford went out to make their sketch for Miss Bennett. He was silent with doubt and anxiety, for he was desperately in love with the girl beside him. There was something almost unreal about her to him. She had come from nowhere, she had no past, no pleasant memories to talk about. All he knew was that Alice had known her for a little while at school, that she had an uncle in Australia, and no home in the world. She was here by a chance, as though she had dropped from the clouds, and she was going—only Heaven knew whither. He felt sometimes as if she were in reality the waif she called herself just passing by. He wanted to stop her, to hold her fast, to take her back to Lahore and give her all the things of which as yet she

seemed to know nothing, and to feel that her
aloneness had made her doubly his.   Meanwhile they walked on with the camp-stools and
the sketching things.   She was silent, too, but
it was from sheer contentment that did not need
words, not even his words, to make it better;
and if she thought beyond the moment, why,
the simple philosophy of the last few days
comforted her.   The sun was shining and the
sky was blue; all about them Nature was at
her best; beside her walked the man she loved.
If she was no longer an unsophisticated girl in
some things—for marriage even such as hers
could hardly leave her that—love was altogether an ideal thing to her, and absolutely
pure and unselfish.   She was glad to love him,
glad that he lived in the world, and exultant
that that sweet summer morning had thrown
them together for a few hours alone on the
mountain-top away from everyone beyond.
And when they went back to the hotel, there
would be his mother, whom she loved too, and
there were still some days to come.   Even

when she had to leave these dear people, she would take with her the remembrance of the wonderful time spent with them, the knowledge that they had liked having her with them, and she would love them just the same always as long as her life went on. She looked up at him : there were tears in her eyes and he saw them.

"Is anything the matter?" he asked.

"No. It is only that it is all so beautiful and I am happy, and wish it could go on always."

"Why shouldn't it?"

"All things must come to an end, or there could be no beginnings."

"That's a paradox or philosophy or something; you didn't pull it off very well." She laughed away her tears.

"It is so difficult to make jokes unless you are used to it.—Nothing could be better than this point for Miss Bennett's sketch. Let us get to work."

They sat down and put their blocks on their

knees, opened their little boxes of colours and
the covered cup of water, and worked for at
least half an hour.

"Well?" he said at last.

"I think we are getting on beautifully."

"So do I—going at it hard. Perhaps they
will put us in the Royal Academy next year."

"Or the Luxembourg."   Another half-
hour.

"Mustn't be too ambitious—a woman always is, though. I'm tired of industry," he
said, and putting away his colours, stood for a
few minutes looking over her shoulder till she,
too, gave up work. Then she turned round
on her stool and waited as if for him to speak.
He took it as an encouragement and gathered
courage. "I wish you would come back to
England." But she shook her head. "Why
not? Do you know," he went on gently, "I
think sometimes that you had a very bad time
when you were a child. Did they bully you?"

"Oh, I don't know. I suppose I was
properly brought up and it was good for me.

I had no other children to play with," she
added, for she did not like to think unkindly
of Uncle Robert. "Perhaps that had something to do with my not being happy ; and,
Jim," she looked up at him with almost an
entreaty in her eyes, " I don't want to go back
to England ; don't let the Mummy ask me any
more——"

" I wish you would come with us ; we
would try to make you happy, Kathy," and
he sat down on the ground by her camp-stool.

" I can't "—something in her heart warned
her that the conversation was becoming dangerous—" I want to spend the winter in
Italy."

" And alone ? " She nodded her head, and
looked away into the distance they had been
sketching. " But, Katherine," and he put his
hand on hers. She started as if she were
afraid, for he was looking at her eagerly.
" Don't be angry," he said in a low voice as
she tried to get up. " I was only going to say
that it is rather odd, you know, for a girl to be

abroad alone, staying about by herself all the
winter."

"Mrs. Carter, at the hotel, is all alone ; she
is not much older than I am."

"She is a married woman.   Besides, we
want you with us."   She tried to laugh away
her embarrassment.

"I can take care of myself," she said.
"Come, let us walk on.   Alice said you were
very strait-laced ; but I won't do anything
wrong, though I am alone.   I wouldn't for the
world," she added, as they gathered up their
things.   There was not a soul within sound ;
even the hotel, a little way below them, was
hidden from sight.   They could see nothing
but the sky line of the mountain range.   They
walked on for a few minutes before he answered.

"I don't believe you would.   I don't think
you would know how.   Will you be glad
when we are gone ? "

"Glad !   Why should I be that, when this
is the happiest time of all my life ? "   The

tears came into her eyes again ; but she turned away so that he should not know.

"And of mine," he said, and put his arm on her shoulder, and drew her a little way towards him and looked at her face. "Yes, let us stop a minute," he went on in a tone that would not be resisted. "Look here, we might lean against this rock, if you do not want to lean against me—and the happiest time of my life too, Kathy. I am so afraid to speak to you, my darling, you have known me such a little while, and perhaps you think I am just a ruffian ; but I love you and want you to stay with me, and to belong to us for ever." She trembled with fright, but she could not keep the happiness out of her heart nor out of her eyes, and he saw it there. "I want you to come back with the Mummy and me, my darling. She loves you, and I love you, my sweet one—I love you better than anyone in all the world." She tried to turn away from him, but perhaps she managed badly, for somehow her head went on his shoulder, and he stooped and

kissed her hair ; and she forgot to consider
whether it was right or wrong—only for a moment.   Then she remembered :

"You mustn't—you mustn't ! "

"Yes, I must," he whispered back, for he
felt that she loved him and was satisfied.   The
rest was only a matter of persuasion.   "I must,
because I love you and want to keep you all
my life.   Do you think you could endure it,
Kathy ? " and he kissed her hair again, and
tried to raise her face to his.   "Could you
marry me and go back to India with me ? "

"Oh, no, no ! " she said, and wrenched herself away.   "You mustn't touch me ; and I
can never marry anybody as long as I live ! "
He looked at her with astonishment ; she had
seemed passive a moment before, and it was
impossible that he could have mistaken the expression in her eyes.

"But I thought you cared for me," he said,
bewildered ; "did I misunderstand ? "

"I do ! " she exclaimed passionately, "I do
care ; it isn't that——"

"And you know that I love you," he said, going forward reassured, but she put out her hand to keep him off.

"No, no!" she cried in alarm; "you mustn't do that—but yes, I know you care for me—I felt it just now."

"Then why won't you let me love you, darling? Why won't you marry me? Is there anyone else?" She hesitated and looked at him, and longed to tell him the truth. But had not Alice said that the Alfords were very proper? And had she not herself heard what the Mummy had said about Mrs. Simpson, the woman who had left her husband? And did not everyone, so far as she knew, agree in thinking that there was but one path to pursue with a runaway wife, and that was to send her back to her husband? Besides, she could not bear to confess that she, who had let him kiss her just now, and had been content and happy to rest her head against him, was a married woman, and had been passing herself off as a girl. He would think her wicked, and despise her. She felt wicked, and despised herself, for, as she stood facing him on the lonely pathway, there rushed back with terrible distinctness the remembrance of her wedding-day and those awful words she had said standing up in church beside Mr. Belcher; she remembered her wedding ring, and signing her name in the vestry, and going away—that terrible going away with Mr. Belcher to Windermere. She thought of Mrs. Oswell, the first person who had ever said "Mrs. Belcher" aloud to her. She could see in imagination the envelopes of the few letters that had come directed to her in her married name, especially the first ones that Mr. Belcher had opened. Everything seemed to stare her in the face as if aghast at what she had done and was doing, and for the first time she felt wicked and deceitful, though she knew that she was neither. He stood looking at her doubtfully, wondering what to do.

"Won't you speak to me, my darling," he

said at last, "and tell me if there is anyone else who cares for you?"

"Anyone else who cares for me!" she repeated. "No, no one in the world, and no one ever did, and I never cared for anyone else." The "else" sent a flash of joy through him. "For anyone else," she said again, as though she knew what it was to him, "in my whole life—and I never shall."

"Then, my. sweet, it is all right," he said, in the happy voice she loved, and that this last hour had seemed to be waking up some new life in her to stir her heart and soul, and he tried to reach her face again. But she drew back with alarm that had more in it than mere shyness.

"You mustn't," she cried, "you mustn't— mustn't."

"But you love me, dear? You said you cared for me. You meant it, didn't you?"

"I love you more than the whole world," she answered. "I think there was never, never anyone like you," and she burst into tears.

"And you are going to marry me, my darling."

"No, I can't," she answered firmly, still carefully keeping him at bay. "I am never going to marry anyone as long as I live."

"Dear goose," he said tenderly, "you are going to marry me."

"No," she cried, and looked at him with the hunted look that puzzled him sorely. "I can't, Jim. I am not going to marry you—I can never marry anybody."

"And you don't care for anyone else," he said, "and no one cares for you, and never did."

"Never—never," she said, and clasped her hands and stood with her head bowed. He looked at her curiously, up and down, almost as if he wondered whether it could really be she herself who stood there.

"Kathy," he said gravely, "I love you with all my heart, and you say you love me, and I want you to be my wife, darling. Won't you?"

"No, I won't," she said very gently, "but I love you," she pleaded.

"It is no use saying that," he answered coldly. "I feel that somehow you are not treating me fairly. Come, let us go." And they walked back to the hotel in silence.

CHAPTER XIV.

She stopped by the steps and looked up at him. "Would you mind," she said gently, "not telling the Mummy before lunch? It has been all so strange and sudden. I don't think I could face her if you did. Let it be till this evening." For answer he nodded his head and lagged behind.

She went up to her own room—that room in which she had thought over many things and lived a lifetime while she looked out at the plains of Lombardy—and shut the door and put her hand to her head and tried to realise whether she was awake or dreaming. So many conflicting emotions beset her that her brain was in a whirl; and yet, almost against her will, her poor human heart beat

for joy. For did not Jim Alford love her best
in the world, and want to marry her—to spend
his whole life with her? Only the terrible
mistake that had been made for her—she had
not made it for herself—stood between her and
that great happiness. But she could not dwell
on the mistake now, for the intoxication of the
moment rose above her knowledge of the im-
possibilities. Never once in her whole life had
she been loved before—her cheeks burnt for
joy and shame together while she remembered
it. Was it wrong? How could it be—this
thing that was true? Neither he nor she
would do anything wrong for the world.

Then she remembered his coldness, and her
heart stood still; perhaps he would refuse to
be friends again—the friends they had been.
She did not think she could bear that. And
yet, for she felt that she must look things in the
face, suppose he did remain distant and angry?
It would break her heart. She could be content knowing that he loved her and disguised
his love with friendship, though they were a

16

thousand miles apart, but not if he were changed towards her. But of course he would change towards her if she declared she loved him and yet refused to marry him. What could he think but that she did not care for him so much as for her liberty, or so much as he did for her—he who wanted her for his whole life? She seemed to live hours while one possibility after another presented itself to her whirling brain. In the first moment of wild excitement she had had an idea that he would forget his proposal after a little while, and go back to the old footing, and they would be closer, happier friends than ever, with the exquisite knowledge at their hearts that they loved each other. "But no, no!" she shook her head, and realised that they could never go back to it. Something in space that was like a whisper from the world told her so. They would remember that morning all their lives, and hunger for more than had before contented them. "And we might have been so happy, life might have been such a wonderful thing!

It is for people who feel as we do that marriage was made, not for cruel or worldly people to gain money or position by," and she burst into passionate tears. "I ought to tell him! It would be fairer—it would be right—even though it kills me, he ought to know!" But her courage failed her as she said it. He would think her so wicked, and never understand how she, a girl who had travelled alone to Italy and unafraid of the world, had been kept down and cowed in the old Shooter's Hill days. He would never understand the insults and sneers, apart from the blows that had brought about the crisis of Montague Place.

Then the Mummy. She would have to know, and had she not said that nothing justified a woman in leaving her husband? They would send her back—the Mummy and Jim—they would despise her and send her back. Perhaps they would think it a duty to write to Mr. Belcher. Her heart grew cold at the thought. She felt that she would rather live any lonely or miserable life that could be de-

vised for her on this earth than go back to Mr.
Belcher. She would infinitely rather die. She
got up and stood by the bed, looking out dismayed into space. The great joy of earth had
come to her—the joy of being loved by the man
to whom her heart was given, but it brought
her only trouble and difficulty ; she had to put
it aside for the sake of a tie that was only an
idea. All trace of her marriage to Mr. Belcher
had vanished so completely from her surroundings, and even from her thoughts of late, that
it had become like a dream to her, or like a
nightmare that would only return to a sleeper
who dared to shut his eyes. "Oh, life is the
strangest thing in the world," she said to herself, and looked out of the window for a moment almost beseechingly, as if asking the
world she saw from it to give her counsel.
Then the door opened, and Miss Bennett
looked in. She was pale and haggard. Katherine saw it with a start, and chokingly pushed
her own interests aside.

"Oh, Miss Bennett !" she said, "I meant

to have gone to you this morning, but we went out early to make that sketch from the top. I fear we didn't get much done," and she looked ruefully at the block she had thrown carelessly on the table; "but I will try and finish it to-morrow. Sit here by the window, you look so very tired."

"I have had a pleasant surprise and wanted to tell you. Never mind about the sketch. I daresay I should only give it away," she added, with her usual lack of graciousness. "I am going from here in a few days—in fact, as soon as I can get away," and a smile broke over her face.

"Something has happened to you," Katherine said wonderingly — "something that pleases you."

"Yes, it has. Perhaps it will please you, too, for you offered to lend me your money."

"I wish you had taken it."

Miss Bennett shook her head. "I couldn't take it from a girl. You may have little enough, for all I know. This morning I had

a letter. Look!" She took a registered envelope from her pocket. It contained bank-
notes for a hundred pounds; on a sheet of
paper that enclosed them were the words,
With best wishes. Katherine felt a throb of
joy go through her, for she understood—Jim
had done it, she was certain of it. She remembered the expression on his face the other
night, when he said that it must be a bad
thing to be dying and stranded; and his
mother had often told her of his easy gener-
osity. Oh, yes, it was he beyond all doubt.
She counted up the days that had intervened—
the days of bad weather—since that talk to
which he had never afterwards alluded. There
had been just time for him to write home and
direct the money to be sent in this manner.
"Yes, it is Jim," she said to herself, while the
tears came into her eyes. "It is like you, and
I am proud of you, and love you. Oh! you
must never know how I have deceived you. I
will go away at once." She almost started at
the idea—it would solve so many difficulties.

Then she stooped and kissed Miss Bennett from sheer gratitude, for had not the sick woman given her the knowledge of this good deed?

" I don't know where they came from," Miss Bennett said. " They may be a gift, or the payment of a debt. I had just fifty pounds left, and had written home for it. Now, perhaps, I shall have enough left, when my bill is paid, to last me till I die."

Someone walked along the corridor outside, half hesitated, and went downstairs. Katherine felt certain that it was Jim ; she knew his step.

" Oh, don't talk of dying," she said gently. " Life is sweet at its worst, and you may get well. Tell me where you are going."

" To Italy. Perhaps I shall live through the winter. When I am much worse my sister will come, but she will not be able to stay long."

Katherine knew what she meant. This planned meeting of life and death made her shudder.

"But where, precisely, are you going?" she asked. "And are you going alone?"

"There is a woman I know—she has a little pension on the Italian Riviera—at Alassio. It is just a little place, and hardly anyone has heard of it. She and I have known each other for years, and she does not talk. I want to be with someone who is silent."

"But you can't go alone?"

"I must, and this money makes it possible."

"Let me take you?" Katherine exclaimed. "I am going from here; I want to go. Oh, do let me take you. I couldn't bear to think of you on your way alone."

"I thought you were going to marry Mrs. Alford's son."

"No, that is impossible; and they are going home very soon. Let me take you to Alassio; I won't talk; I will be very silent. And I want to go to some little Italian place—that has been my intention, but it must be a place where there are no English at all. Perhaps I might find one near you ; then I should see you sometimes in the winter."

"I should like to see you ; you are a good girl, and mean well," Miss Bennett said, and Katherine heard her with infinite gratitude. "There is an hotel half a mile out of Alassio, low down on the shore. It has an orange garden, the largest one I know, and the mountains rise up beyond. It might do for you, and I have heard that it is cheap: women who are alone never have any money," she added with grim sarcasm. "Or. a mile farther on is Laigueglia. There are no English there, and very few Italians—only a cracked white marble church, a few ruined houses, and desolate gardens."

"When shall you be ready to go ?"

Miss Bennett answered quickly: "Directly —in a day or two—as soon as I have packed my things ; they will not take long—there are only those two little boxes. But if you can't be ready so soon I will wait. After all, it

doesn't matter," and her momentary excitement died away.

" I will tell you after lunch, or at tea-time
if that will do, when I can be ready." Katherine followed the direction of Miss Bennett's
eyes and saw Jim Alford taking the downward
path towards Mendrisio. "Perhaps he is going away to avoid me," she thought, catching
her breath. "I will go when you like," she
said, turning to Miss Bennett. "Hark! there
is the luncheon bell. Let us go down," she
cried eagerly.

Mrs. Alford was taking her place at table.

"Has Jim gone away?" Katherine asked
breathlessly.

"No, my dear," the old lady said, looking
up with mild surprise; "he has only gone out
for a couple of hours because he wanted to be
alone. He will be back by three o'clock; but
he talks of going to Milan for a few days.
I wish he would wait for me," she added.
"This is quite a sudden freak."

" I will go first," Katherine thought.

CHAPTER XV.

"But, my dear," Mrs. Alford said bewildered, "Jim will be miserable when you are gone, and so shall I." This was a couple of hours after lunch, while they sat together in the sitting-room that had gradually become home-like.

"You will have him to take care of you," Katherine answered; "he has only a few months more to be with you. They will be better without a third person, dear Mummy; and I must journey on. Some day I shall see you again, I hope."

"But you may not see him again for years."

"I know," she said, in a voice that she could not keep steady, for though she had faced this possibility in her own room, it was harder to hear it put into words—they brought her knowledge of how difficult it would be to tear her life away from his. What! never to see him again or to hear his laugh, or walk beside him, or to read Browning—had he not told her how dangerous it was? He was going back to England and then to India, and she—Heaven alone knew where; and the beginning of this state of things was only a day or two distant: it came upon her with an overwhelming sense that was not to be borne. She could not live entirely without him. They must be friends, very great friends. Nothing else was possible, and even that was almost impossible while the secret of her life remained one. "I don't suppose," she went on in a dazed voice, "I shall ever see him again after I leave here."

"Tell me," said the old lady, taking her hands and trying to look into her face, "tell me why you are going—is my boy nothing to you? I have been hoping that you were a great deal to each other."

Katherine hesitated for a moment, and then answered simply and out of a full heart, "I think there is no one in the wide world like him, but it can't make any difference, Mummy dear. I can never go to England again while I live."

"Were you treated so very cruelly, my child?"

"I was very miserable there," she answered, and she thought: "Oh, if I could only tell her —if I could only tell her! But she would never forgive me; and she would send me back."

"But your uncle is in Australia?"

"It makes no difference, Mummy!" for latterly she had quite dropped the more formal address. "I want you to promise me something—it is, not to tell anyone in England that you ever met anyone called by my name."

"My dear, what do you mean?"

"Only—if I were discovered I should die; that is why I cannot go back."

"You are not giving me all your confidence," the old lady said gravely.

"No, and I cannot." There was almost agony in her voice. "I have learnt many things in this last year," she went on, "and one is, that people are judged not by the intention in their conduct, but by its effect."

"I do not understand you, my dear," and Mrs. Alford drew back coldly.

"Oh, don't, don't!" Katherine cried. "Love me a little while longer; I am going away in two or three days! Only while I am here, Mummy dear, so that the memory of it is not spoilt—won't you?" She took the old lady's hands and kissed them. "I always told you that I was a waif; perhaps you had better forget all about me when I go, as you would about a waif who has gone on into the distance or the crowd. Oh, here is Jim! Jim," she said excitedly, "Mummy is angry with me," and she put her arms round the old lady's neck and kissed her. "This dear Mummy, who has been so kind to me, kinder than anyone else in the wide world, and given me more happiness than I ever knew in all my life before—enough to last me all my life. I have not done any harm, dear Mummy, I have not indeed—you needn't look so coldly at me. Jim," she said, turning to him quickly, "I want to talk to you all by myself. I may, may I not, dear Mummy? Shall we go to the farm once more, you and I, and get the cream for tea? They will want their tea, you know, Jim, and we sha'n't be able to go again, for I am going away——"

"Going away!"

"Yes, with Miss Bennett. I will tell you on the way to the farm. Oh, do let us go," she pleaded, for she fancied that he hesitated, "just for a last, last time along the little pathway. I will get my hat at once." She put her cheek lovingly against the old lady's for a moment, then fled along the corridor.

"Jim," Mrs. Alford said to her son, "I think I know that child's secret: the Ogre ill-treated her and she ran away."

"Well, he is safe in Australia now—and I'll try what I can do this afternoon."

"I am ready, I am quite ready," Katherine said, appearing at the doorway. He crossed over to her quickly and they set off together, down the stairs and out of the hotel and towards the farm. "You are angry, I know you are angry," she said, still speaking breathlessly; "you and the Mummy are both changing to me at the same moment."

"Changing!" he said, "when only this morning I told you how much I loved you." He turned and looked at her, and she saw the expression on his face and faltered.

"And I love you, Jim, dear," she said, looking back at him with her blue eyes full of tears. "And I love you, God knows I do, only indeed you mustn't ask me to marry you."

He shook his head. "You are not treating me fairly, Kathy," he said tenderly, but she knew by his tone that he meant what he said.

"But can't you feel that I love you, can't you hear it in my voice, don't you know it?" she asked desperately.

"I do," he said, "and that makes it all the more strange."

"Doesn't it satisfy you, as the knowledge of your love shall satisfy me? Why must it be marriage or nothing at all?" and she drew closer to him, for they were on the narrow pathway going towards the farm, and not a soul was within sight nor sound of them. "Why can't we be friends—very dear friends —all our lives? We might be just like brother and sister—you never had a sister of your very own——"

"Nonsense," he said, and put his arm round her shoulder, but she shook it off quickly. "People cannot be brothers and sisters, my child, when they are in love with each other."

"Oh, but they can; and they can be friends. Think how much better it would be than nothing—nothing! And if we can't

17

marry, and we can't—for I don't want to be married, and can't be; and it is better to be free—we might be friends." She was almost incoherent with nervousness. "Very dear friends—we could always be that—and we could write to each other very often, and tell each other everything we did and thought and read, and be everything in the world that two people parted by long miles can be."

"All this is nonsense, Kathy. You don't know what you are talking about, my darling. What you say may be all very well for two friends who desire to be nothing more; but you and I love each other—at least I know that I love you with all my heart," he said simply. "I want you to come to me, to share my life, to be with me always. And if you loved me you would want it too."

They were within sight of the farm, and stopped and looked at each other; then sat down on the little bank beside the pathway.

"I love you, and I do want it too," she said earnestly. "But I cannot marry you, and—I think," she added, bursting into passionate tears, "that marriage is the most hateful and terrible thing in the world."

"Well, that is rather an odd thing to hear the woman you love best in the world say."

"I mean the ceremony that binds you so that you can never get away, no matter how much you hate each other, nor how miserable you are together. If you love each other and promise to be faithful all your lives"—she stood up in her excitement and looked at him —"promise with your whole heart and soul, oughtn't that to bind you? And yet it doesn't. People talk of making their vows before God—doesn't God hear you when you are alone?"

"Katherine," he said, staring at her with astonishment, "I don't understand this outburst. What on earth has make you think so much about the marriage ceremony?"

"Because I hate it," she said. "Because it is an excuse to bind two people together who want to be separate, and it fetters them when they want to be free. Jim," she went on in a whisper while a flush dyed her face, "is not this morning—should not the memory of it be enough to satisfy us? We can never get away from it or forget it as long as we live. Isn't it much more than the bond between two people who have stood up in church together and said things they did not mean? Don't you think God heard us just as much saying the things we did mean as he would have heard two people saying the things they did not mean? And which do you think would be marriage in his eyes?"

"I do not understand you," he answered. "You are talking nonsense, and not very pleasant nonsense, my child. The marriage ceremony may be only the public record of the vows that people have made each other in private; but it was made by the strong for the protection of the weak, and the strong must protect it. I have no sympathy with fads about marriage nor with any crusade against those things that experience has taught men to be best for the majority. Come, let us go." He turned towards the farm, and with burning cheeks she followed him.

The bottle was filled with cream for the afternoon tea. They refused the bowls of cream the milkmaid offered them, and turned on their way homeward in silence.

"It is the oddest thing in the world," he thought, "that she should go off her head about the marriage ceremony. Some women are rather too eager for it. Perhaps the Ogre wasn't happy in his domestic relations." Somehow her talk had repelled him. He liked a woman who reverenced forms and ceremonies ; he even liked her to be a little superstitious. "What put all that stuff in your head about marriage ?" he asked ; "you couldn't have spoken more vehemently if you had had a drunken husband who beat you every Saturday night."

"Ah," she said eagerly, "now you have touched it. Suppose a woman has a drunken husband who beats her on Saturday nights, a man she doesn't love and has never loved, but has married for some other reason; or if a man has a bad and wicked woman for a wife, not a woman he has once loved, and so for the sake of that remembrance is willing to bear with, are they to stay together and be miserable all their lives?"

."Yes, I think so," he answered slowly; "if they had not cared for each other they should not have married——"

"Oh, yes, yes; I agree in that."

"But having done so, no matter for what reason, I think they are bound to remain together if it is in any way possible, for the more terrible, the more sacred, and the more binding you can make marriage, so gradually will you increase the respect for it. I neither believe in easy marriage nor in easy divorce myself. Just as the soldier is sacrificed for the battle, so must the everyday individual be sacrificed for the sake of the institution that has been found to work best and to be best for the majority. Katherine," he said suddenly, "I hope you haven't been talking with any of the unpleasant women who tell you that men are wicked and that women are men's superiors, and all the rest of it ?"

"No," answered Katherine, wonderstruck, "I don't even know what you mean. I think men and women too, as a rule, are very dear and good. All that I have known or seen, with one exception"—and her lips turned white, but still he was unsuspicious, "have been. Men and women are just as good as each other, it seems to me, though, of course, the men are stronger and wiser than the women—at least," she said, looking up with the quick smile he loved, "it's nicer when they are ; it makes them able to take care of us: I can't think of anything better in the world than being taken care of by anyone— the man," she added shyly, "you love best in the world."

"And you don't know ten thousand people who have all married miserably ?" he asked

joyously, for it seemed as if things were coming round to the point he wished.

"No," she said, with a little sorry laugh,
"I knew of one miserable marriage, but the
others," and she thought of the Oswells and
of George and Alice Alford, "have been perfectly happy. In England I used to walk
about alone and look at the people two and
two, always a man and a woman, and think
how glad they seemed to be together."

"As we will be, my sweet, when we are
married," he said, and made a sudden snatch
as if to take her in his arms and kiss her.

"Oh, no," she cried, "never as long as
we live!" and in her fright she dropped the
bottle of cream out of her. basket. It fell at
their feet and was broken. They looked at it
in silence for a moment, and swift as lightning
her thoughts went back to the day when she
had dropped the bowl of flowers. It had always seemed to her, in looking back, that
upon that day her childhood ended; it flashed
upon her that perhaps on this day too there

ended something in her life—something that would never come again.

He looked up and met her eyes. "Never mind the cream," he said, almost indignantly, "that does not matter, but I do not understand you, Katherine. Do you mean to say that it can never be?"

"No, never," she answered. "But cannot we be friends?" she pleaded.

"No, we cannot," he answered decisively. "That means—at worst, what I do not even choose to mention to you——"

"But, at best?"

"Something that may be satisfactory for one, but never is for two. I shall go away to-morrow or the next day," he said curtly, as they entered the hotel, but she made no answer, only looked round at him as they went upstairs.

"I am going to lie down," she said, "and shall not come in to dinner to-night, but I will see you both afterwards in the sitting-room; perhaps there will be a fire," she added, with a little shiver, as she disappeared from his sight. Then she went into her room once more, and sat down feeling that she had only made him love her less, and widened the distance between them. "It is no good," she thought bitterly; "my life is my own; I have to suffer all its pain, and yet I cannot fashion it as I like. I might as well try to shape water with my hands. A little life like mine, too. The secret of the world seems to be that one has to submit to the powers that are stronger than oneself; no matter how much one's heart longs to fight them, and it's the most terrible thing on earth to do wrong, for sin is like a ball passing from hand to hand, changing its shape and colour as it goes along. If only Richard Morris had not done wrong Uncle Robert would not have been so stern, nor have married me to Mr. Belcher; and if Mr. Belcher had not been cruel I should not have run away and deceived the Mummy and Jim." She stood up and considered it, looking out at the plains in the distance. "I think I understand," she said to

herself at last. "The great laws of life are
our masters and avenge themselves terribly on
those who dare to tamper with them. Only I .
have been so happy," she went on, a little
gratitude coming into her eyes, "and I don't
care—I don't care what comes of it. I have
had a flash of summer right across my life. I
should never have known it if I had not come
here or if they had known. Oh! think,
think!" she exclaimed, clasping her hands,
"what it would have been to have lived all my
life and to have loved no one. I ought to be
very thankful for this that has come into my
heart." A sudden idea smote her as though it
came from Heaven. "And I will make it a
thank-offering," she said slowly, "a thank-
offering that shall try me sorely and cost me
much, but I will do it as a proof of the
strength of the love I bear him." She sat
down still and silent for half an hour ; a great
resolution took possession of her, and she determined that nothing should tempt her to go
from it.

She got up and made some tea for Miss Bennett.

"Miss Kerr," the sick woman said, "these people downstairs are very inattentive, though I have paid their bill. I shall leave to-morrow morning, and have ordered the chair to carry me down and the mule for my baggage. If you could come a day later, I would wait for you at Mendrisio?"

It was an unexpected stroke of good fortune. "But I will go with you to-morrow," she exclaimed, "as early as you like, and gladly."

CHAPTER XVI.

Mrs. Alford was alone when Katherine went to her after dinner. Jim had gone for a stroll by himself: it was a sign of the changed state of things that he had done so.

"He will be back directly," his mother said apologetically, and sat down by the fire and warmed her hands in silence. Katherine crouched on a low stool at her feet, and watching the crackling wood. Presently she looked up.

"Mummy," she said, "while you were at dinner I put all your things tidy, and your tea-basket is back in your room. Is there anything else I can do for you this evening? To-morrow I am going away with Miss Bennett." She kissed the old lady's hand as if to soften the news of her sudden departure.

"To-morrow!"

"Yes, to-morrow," Katherine repeated sadly. "There is no one else to take care of her. She needs me ; you have Jim."

"He needs you too. I don't know what there is in your heart, my dear, except that it is something you are keeping from me. I think you might have trusted me. I have been very fond of you."

"And I of you, dear Mummy."

"Then why should you go? You said you were fond of Jim : I hoped you were, but he has told me about this afternoon. He never loved any other woman in his life—I thought you cared for him."

"I do," she whispered. "I love him with all my heart, and think there is no one like him in the world. The mere sound of his step makes my heart beat, and to hear his voice and see his face are life and happiness to me."

"Then why don't you marry him, my darling?" the old lady said, taking her in her arms.

"I can't, I can't," and she crouched down on her stool again and looked into the fire.

Then Jim entered, and Mrs. Alford turned to him quickly, longing to bring about an acute crisis of some sort. "Katherine is going away to-morrow," she said, "she·and Miss Bennett together."

"To-morrow?" he echoed.

"Yes, and I want to say good-bye to-night, so waited till you came." Then she turned to his mother, "You have been very kind to me, Mummy. I can't thank you now, but I will all my life when I think of you." She had risen from her stool and stood looking at them both.

Mrs. Alford took her hands and held them. "You have been very kind to me," she said, "except in going from me. Why won't you stay, and why can't you make my son happy?" Then Katherine stooped and kissed her, and drew her hands away and crossed to the door, which was shut. She had not spoken to Jim, who waited awkwardly by the table in the middle of the room, but she gave him a quick look, and as she did so he saw that her face was pale, and her eyes had a strange hunted look in them.

"Kathy," he said, "I didn't mean the Mummy to say that to you, or that you should be troubled again in any way. Say good-bye to me, my dear, and God bless you." He went towards her and held out his hand. She motioned him back, and stood half hesitating with her back against the door, and faced him and the old lady.

"Wait," she said, evidently speaking with difficulty, "I want to tell you before I go, though you will never speak to me again; but I made up my mind this afternoon when we came back from the farm that you should know the truth. It is better than anything else—I make it my thank-offering for the happiness of the past months." She spoke hurriedly, as if she were afraid lest her courage should fail before she finished. "It is not because I don't want to stay with you that I am going, or because—or because I don't love Jim.

If I didn't it would not matter. He is more than the whole world to me." He made a step forward, but she put up her hands as if to keep him back. "I am going away because—I—I am married to somebody else."

"You are married!" the old lady exclaimed, while Jim looked at her as though he thought she were mad.

"Yes, I am married," she said with a gasp of relief at having brought it out at last. "I was made to marry, but Uncle Robert did it for the very best, I know he did," she added gently. "He thought that every woman ought to be married. I had no relations, and he was afraid of leaving me alone in the world. I know he did it for the best," she shuddered; "he meant to be kind; but I was miserable, for I didn't love the man, I never did for a single moment; but I was powerless and helpless, and had been brought up to think that women were obliged to do as men told them. It seems so weak and foolish to me now since I have realised that we have each to live our own

18

lives and to choose the great things in them for ourselves."

"But whom did you marry?" Mrs. Alford asked, bewildered.

"A friend of Uncle Robert's," Katherine answered, speaking in the manner of a hunted woman who had been brought to bay at last. "I had known him since I was a little girl. He was a great deal older than I—eighteen years, I think—and I didn't want to marry him, and told him so."

"Was he so much in love with you?" Jim asked.

"No," she answered sadly, shaking her head. It would be mean and ungenerous, she thought, seeing that Mr. Belcher was not there to defend himself, to explain wholly how cruel he had been—besides, her pride would not let her confess his blows. But some things she felt bound to say in self-defence. "No, he was not in love with me, but he knew that Uncle Robert wished to see me married—and he knew I should have Uncle Robert's money.

He married me for that. I had no will of my own in anything, and no one to consult—no mother or sisters or friends, no one in the world except Uncle Robert, who had had a great trouble about his son. It made him very unhappy, and he grew silent and morose, and very stern, so that he hardly took any notice of me." She said it gently, as if to soften her words. "There was no one else except Susan, who said that men were the stronger race, and that women must obey them. Oh, you can't understand, you can't indeed," she cried, clasping her hands, and looking up at Jim. "I could not help myself in any way ; I felt like a prisoner who was bound and had been born bound. It never even occurred to me to make a desperate struggle for freedom. I made a little feeble one, but it was useless."

"But when were you married?" Mrs. Alford asked, still bewildered, for Katherine's story sounded so impossible. "You were so very young."

"I was eighteen—it was the most dreadful

day of my life—and that is what I meant," she
went on, turning to Jim, "about the marriage
ceremony.   Why should words I did not mean
or say willingly bind me?   And why should he
be able without offence to any law at all to
marry me, not because he wanted me but because he wanted Uncle Robert's money?   There
is something very wrong somewhere that such
a thing should be possible," she said passionately.   "It ought to be the bitterest sin, the
most terrible disgrace, to marry for any reason
on earth except because you want to spend
your whole lives together, and care for each
other with all your hearts."

"That is the only reason an honest man
does marry," he exclaimed.

"I have thought about it so much," she
went on vehemently, as if she had not heard
him, "hour after hour as I sat in the next
room looking across the plains of Lombardy.
People who would be afraid to cheat or com-
mit crimes for which they would be put in
prison will take a false oath in a church and

say things they do not dream of meaning, and never seem to have it on their conscience. Is it because they think God will not tell their fellow-men, or does not hear them, or because they think that truth and honour have little to do with marriage?"

"Katherine!" Mrs. Alford exclaimed, looking at her with astonishment.

"Yes, Mummy," the girl continued breathlessly, "I have thought and thought till I have been nearly mad. People ought to hesitate and think a great deal—unless they love each other so much that there can be no doubt at all about it—before they vow their whole lives to each other. I think each one should go alone and make a declaration before some official that they want to marry, so that they are very sure of themselves. Even if they are not terribly in love—perhaps all people cannot be—they ought to like each other best in the world and want to be together. And the ceremony should be the most sacred thing on earth—the most binding and the most blessed—and nothing should undo it, not even death, between people who have been faithful and happy together and loved each other all the time. When one dies, the other should die too, or else should live doing what the other had left undone. But now, marriage, on which one's whole happiness depends, is a careless, easy thing, done for money or from fear, or because of a sudden fancy, as if it lasted a month instead of a life-time, and it is a mere chance whether it makes for joy or sorrow—just a toss-up."

"But all marriages are not as you say," Mrs. Alford said coldly, and still bewildered by Katherine's confession.

"No, dear Mummy, they are not, but many are; and even one in a town should be a dis-grace—like murder. It is worse than murder, for it lasts longer. Mr. Belcher married me because he wanted Uncle Robert's money, not because he loved me; and I married him be-cause I was helpless and afraid of Uncle Robert; and I was young—only a school-girl —and no companion for him, and he was none for me. We were just two strangers living in the same house. I was in his way, as a stranger is; he resented it when he saw me, and lived his own life, so far as he could, without me."

"Why didn't you try to love him?" Mrs. Alford asked sternly. "He was your husband."

"I did, I did!" she said in a despairing tone, "but it was useless. All my life I had been afraid of him, had never even liked him. I can't explain what life was with him. Perhaps it was all my fault—only I know this, that I was the most miserable girl in the wide world. One day," she went on quickly, "he told me he was going away for a week. He had been very cruel——"

"Cruel?" repeated Jim in a low voice.

"Yes," answered Katherine. "Perhaps I ought not to say things against him while he is not here, but he was cruel—cruel, and he went away. I was nearly mad and hated him—I never did anything else but hate him and

shudder at his voice. When he had gone—
Uncle Robert had started for Australia—I ran
away. Yes, I did, Mummy," and the tears
ran down her face. "Uncle Robert gave me
some money before he went to Australia, and
Mrs. Barrett left me some, and I ran away.
That was how you found me on board ship.
Alice never guessed I was married. I had
thrown my wedding-ring into the sea——"

"You should have told me," Mrs. Alford
said.

"I couldn't. I was afraid. I have thought
sometimes," she went on, for she reproached
herself concerning Mr. Belcher now that she
had put his conduct into words, "that he
meant to be kinder after we were married ; but
he was so much older, and I was such a schoolgirl in mind, and he knew that I did not love
him, for I had told him so, and gradually he
learnt to hate me because he couldn't get rid of
me—that was what I meant, to-day, Jim," she
said, turning to him again. "I don't mean to
scoff at marriage, but I never felt that I was

married to Mr. Belcher at all, and I don't now, only that I was his prisoner, and I can't feel that I have been very wicked except in not telling you before."

"You told me that you loved my son," Mrs. Alford said.

"Yes, dear Mummy, and I do," she answered in a low, sweet voice. "I love him with all my heart, and shall as long as I live—but I would not say it if I ever meant to see him again after to-night. I thought we could be friends, but I see now that he is right in saying that it is impossible. You must not think," she added as Mrs. Alford made a gesture of indignation, "that I mean any harm, for I think the greatest insult to love is to deface it with wickedness. And Jim was quite right to-day when he said we were all bound to respect those laws that were found to work best for mankind, and that each individual must abide by them, no matter how hard they are ; just as a soldier must die in battle for the sake of his country. I have expressed it all so badly, but I have thought about it, and thought about it day and night, and I will try and do what is right always, for the sake of you and Jim."

"Then, my dear," said Mrs. Alford solemnly, "you will let your husband know your whereabouts?"

Poor Katherine's heart called out dumbly, "Oh, I knew, I knew she would say it!" But she answered firmly, "No, Mummy, I cannot."

"No, of course she can't," said Jim indignantly, and then he turned to Katherine. "My darling," he said, "everything is, and must be, at an end between us in one way, but I shall love you as long as I live, and we will try to be friends or like brother and sister," he added desperately.

"No," she answered, shaking her head. "That cannot be now. I do not think," she added in a whisper, " that it would satisfy me. I want you to love me so much, much more that it would be wrong—it is better that we should be strangers—just hearing from each other now and then," she added wistfully.

"It's such a frightful puzzle, such a hole for you to be in, my poor darling."

"You mustn't call me that," she said in a tone of happy fright. "If you only won't think badly of me, that is all I want. And if I love you when you are in India—so far away as that, it will seem like a religion and become beautiful. Talk it all over with the Mummy, Jim dear, and when you have thought it out, perhaps you or she will write to me." And before they knew what she was going to do she had opened the door and vanished from their sight.

CHAPTER XVII.

ALASSIO is a very little place on the Italian Riviera, half-way between Savona and San Remo. Inside the town gates are only a couple of narrow streets, worn into ruts like the streets of Pompeii, hardly wide enough to let two well-loaded donkeys pass each other comfortably, a little square market-place, a few primitive shops, and a couple of hotels that have seen better days. Beyond the gates are two or three fairly new hotels, the old picturesque church with its square towers, a few villas, and, a little way above them, the Protestant church built by a handful of devout English. Dotted about on the mountain sides at irregular intervals are more villas, and here and there a shrine or ruined chapel. In and

out the olive woods towards Albenga, the next
town to Alassio, winds a narrow Roman road,
along which Hannibal is said to have led his
followers into Southern Italy.

But though Alassio is a pleasant enough
place to the idler or the invalid, or to the
romantic in search of the picturesque, it has
no attractions for the frivolous or fashionable.
When Katherine and Miss Bennett journeyed
there, it was known to very few English folk,
and they kept its beauty a secret to themselves. It is on one side of a bay, as if it had
dropped there gracefully and quite by accident; and a little way off—a mile or two, perhaps—is the village of Laigueglia, which might
be Alassio's only child keeping respectfully at
a distance from its parent. These two have
the bay to themselves, and all along the shore
are really fine sands on which the children
seek for Venus's slippers, and play among the
boats and the brown sails and fishing-nets
hung out to dry. Close behind, in a grand
semicircle are the mountains; there is no plain

between them and the sea, save the sands and
as much ground as is necessary for the little
town to stand upon, and there is no visible
break in their chain.　Besides the sand and
the sea and the mountains there are the olive-
woods and the maidenhair valley, and the
Banxia roses and the red berries of the sarsa-
parilla, and the acacia carubas, which are
especially fine, and the palms and the pepper-
trees and the oranges that grow thick as apples
in Devonshire, and the lemons thriving so well
that five millions of them are gathered every
year in the district.　And there are bits of
colour and patches of light, and bells that ring
by fits and starts, and clocks that strike at odd
moments, and a few well-to-do Italians, and
many peasant folk, pleasant to talk with and
picturesque to look at—all these, with the sunshine everywhere, make up the beauty of
Alassio.

At the end towards Albenga, Miss Crockett
kept a little pension in a villa that looked like
a Swiss chalet.　It was almost the last house

in Alassio, and had a garden full of orange-trees and pepper-trees, and geraniums that grew half as high as a man. Behind were the sands and the sea, and in front was a high road. On the other side of the road was a mountain covered with olive woods and crowned by a ruined church that had a history about a princess who had built it as a thank-offering for having married her lowly born lover. To the right stretched the white Corniche road on its way to Albenga and the towns beyond; and to the left it went past the villas and the church and the Grand Hotel, and the turning to the station, on to the town gates, through the town and out by the gates, at the other end, past an hotel built low down on the water's edge, and on, beside the railway line and the great yellow sands and the blue sea, to Laigueglia.

Miss Bennett was staying at Miss Crockett's pension. The two women had known and dis-liked each other all their lives. They had both been governesses. Miss Bennett had

broken down from ill-health; Miss Crockett
had done the same years before, but she was
better, and had been helped by some old pupils
to start the pension by which she managed to
make a living. She was never sure of filling
all her rooms, so was glad to take Miss Bennett
even at a moderate price, and Miss Bennett
thought it was better to be with her than with
a stranger. She had never pretended to like
Miss Crockett or to hold to her methods of
teaching, so she knew that too much civility
would not be expected of her. Thus it was
they came together with a certain amount of
congratulation, but with little sympathy on
either side. Miss Bennett's strength seemed
to be vanishing with the year : she gave more
trouble than other boarders, but by way of
compensation she ate less. The soft Italian
air was doing her good and putting her into a
friendly humour with the world—though not
with its people—before she said good-bye.
Her room was a front one facing the roadway
and the mountain ; for those that faced the

sea at the back were dearer and beyond her
means; she could see the trains flashing
among the olive woods at the foot of the
mountain when she sat at the window—the
train from the Italian frontier going on to
Genoa, and the train from Genoa going back
to the frontier. The people in them were seeking health or pleasure; it was always the same
story, just as it had been at Generoso. She
used to look at them grudgingly, wondering
who was left to work, and who sat still to sorrow, for the world about her seemed to be
given up to pleasure-taking or leisure. Well,
it didn't matter. Soon she would be away
from it all, and the world might go on as
it pleased. She had enough money, Miss
Crockett was not likely to over-charge or
neglect her, Katherine came to see her every
day: she liked Katherine, liked her better
lately since her face had grown white and thin
and very sad. A grim satisfaction came into
her eyes as she noticed it: the girl was being
made to pay, she thought, as all people who

19

lived in the world and dared to bid for happiness were made to pay at some time.

"Is there nothing more I can do—nothing, nothing else?" she would ask Miss Bennett before she left her till the morrow. And the answer was always the same.

"No, thank you, and it would be better to get used to having nothing at all done for me, I don't want to be sorry to die."

"Ah, we must all be that while the sun shines and the trees have leaves and there is a sky above our heads. I think sometimes I would rather live in the bitterest pain than be dead," Katherine said one day.

"The next world may be better."

"But I long for a share of happiness in this one."

"Ah," answered Miss Bennett grimly, "we all do ; but some of us die of hunger. I think you shall go now," she added, "but it does me good to see you come in of a day. I can't think why you wouldn't stay here."

"I will if you like," Katherine answered,

" if it will please you." It was saying a great
deal, and she knew it, but her heart ached so
much for the dying woman that she would
have done anything in the world to give her a
moment's pleasure. It haunted her day and
night, as a sort of refrain to her own life and
its anxieties, that Miss Bennett was dying,
that every day she was a little nearer to the
end that was already well in sight. She had
never beheld death, but now instinctively she
recognised it, and saw its marks upon Miss
Bennett's grey face, and in her eyes that had
grown large and bright and eager, and her
hands that were transparent, and her footsteps
that lagged feebly one after the other with
a pause between, as though the grim shadow
stooped and measured them.

Miss Bennett considered Katherine's question. "No," she answered, "I think you had
better stay where you are. I know the people
here now, and it breaks the day better when
you come in the afternoon. You are a good
girl. I often wonder why you didn't marry

young Alford. Women should marry if they
get the chance. It's a terrible thing when you
grow old to feel that you have missed the near
relationships of life. People who have done
that are only in the way. Besides, women
grow spiteful as they grow old if they are not
married, just as men grow obstinate and narrow if they are alone; each sex needs the
other to leaven it. It is better to be with a
disagreeable man than to grow disagreeable
yourself!"

"Oh, don't let us talk of that; you don't
know how impossible it all is. I wish I could
do something more for you before I go, I do
so little!" But Miss Bennett had closed her
eyes, and did not hear. Katherine, seeing
that she was comfortable, left the room softly
and took her way back to her own lodging.

She was living at Laigueglia, and was the
only Englishwoman in the village, which Miss
Bennett had described well enough—a little,
quiet street, a white marble church cracked by
earthquake, a railway station at which a train

stopped once or twice a day, and a few de-
serted-looking houses with gardens full of
orange-trees; that was all. She had persuaded a woman who kept a little shop to let
her have a bed-room and to provide her with
the morning coffee and the midday meal; the
rest she managed, with the help of a spirit-
lamp and some tea and biscuits, to arrange for
herself.

And here, alone from every one who even
spoke her tongue, she tried to face the prob-
lem of life and the future. She had plenty of
money at the present rate to last her a year
or two. The place was beautiful enough, the
Mediterranean and the mountains and the
wonderful vegetation were intoxicating; but
they were not enough to satisfy her. "I
want more," she cried to herself; "I can't go
on for ever living like this, or measure my
thoughts and longings by the rule of right and
wrong. I want to live, not merely to eat and
drink and take up room in the world and do
nothing—nothing at all. I am of no use at

all now unless it is to poor Miss Bennett, and
she will be gone soon; if I were dead no one
would care, hardly anyone would even know.
Yes, Jim would be sorry, and perhaps the
Mummy." She sat down on the beach half-
way between the hotel, low down on the
water's edge, of which Miss Bennett had told
her, and Laigueglia. The hotel was a long,
rambling building, picturesque enough, with a
great orange garden to it, and immediately behind the mountains rose up high and suddenly
towards the blue sky. Hardly any one stayed
at the hotel, and the few who did were Italians. A man and a woman were sitting in the
garden when Katherine passed, but she had
only seen them in the distance. They came
out from among the orange-trees now and
walked round to the front of the hotel, and
stopped as if they were watching the sunset.
Something made Katherine think that they
were English, but she could not see them well,
and since the man was certainly not Mr.
Belcher, whom she dreaded, or Jim Alford,

for whom she longed, she went on with her own thoughts, idly stirring the sand with her fingers. She felt that somehow she must see Jim again; she loved him more and more every day of her life. All space was empty; every sound seemed to echo in a desert; the hours dragged by and made themselves felt to the uttermost second of every minute. Beautiful; oh, yes! the place might be beautiful, but it was an empty paradise, and she was miserable. All sorts of desperate things she might have done presented themselves to her. "I wish I had never told," she cried, while the blue water surged up to her feet as if to listen. "I might have married him and gone away to India and been happy all my my life and never discovered. It wasn't as if he had been going to live in England. Why didn't I think of it and dare it? I know I could have made him happy, and he would never, never have known. It would have done no one any harm; how can a deed that only makes people happy and does no one any harm be wrong? I can't understand it. But I know this, that I would live a year in prison darkness or bitterest pain for just one hour more with him, and I shall never see him again as long as I live. I used to think that the mere fact of loving him and thinking of him would be enough; but it isn't. I want to see him, and hear him, and to walk beside him. Oh, how wicked I am!—for I want him to kiss me again, and it is all over for ever and ever, and I have to live to the end of my life as best I can. If we had only been like those two people," she thought, as she watched the strangers saunter back to the orange-trees, "they look like Adam and Eve going into the Garden of Eden. It has always been a man and woman—a man and a woman—since the world began. But I have to wander on and be alone always, that is my portion, and some day I shall be old and discontented, waiting for death like Miss Bennett, and have had nothing in life to satisfy me, and be hungry and longing still. Jim will marry somebody else in time—oh, to think of him married to someone else—someone who has always been happy and will be happier still when he loves her, and she goes to spend her whole life with him—makes me feel as if I want to die before it comes to pass." She stood up and looked at the sea—it seemed full of infinite wisdom and understanding. "How foolish I must seem to you!" she cried, holding out her arms towards it. "But I am so miserable! I want to belong to Jim, to be his wife, to spend all my days with him, and to be buried in the same grave with him at last: the chance was mine, but those awful words that I said, just for lack of courage to run away from Uncle Robert, have made it impossible for ever. It will never be now—never—never. I might as well try to walk across you to the horizon in the distance." She turned away with a long sigh, and walked on towards Laigueglia, thinking of the Mummy's letter; for she had written to Mrs. Alford soon after she had arrived at Laigueglia. There had been a fortnight's long

waiting before the answer came, and when it
did, though it was kind enough, it was firm in
its opinion that she ought to go back to her
husband, or to write to her uncle in Australia,
asking him to arrange a separation that was
legal. " *Or, if you like*," the letter went on,
"*and have not courage to do it before, as I
think you ought, come to me at the end of
January, when Jim has gone. I shall be at
Chilworth, and if you like to tell your husband to meet you under my roof, I will do my
best to help you to some arrangement with
him.*" How merciless it seemed: she had no
heart to answer it. Other reference to Jim, except that one about his going, there had been
none in it, but the letter was dated from Milan,
and Katherine divined that they were on their
way back to England. More than a month
had passed since it came, but she could not
think of it calmly: it made her determine that
when Miss Bennett was gone she would journey on to some other place that had no memory of the morning that brought it.

She could not go indoors yet, it was too early. An idea struck her. She would go back to Alassio, through the little town, out at the other end and on to Santa Croce, and see the moon rise through a ruined doorway— all that was left of some old church or monastery—hidden among the woods high up above Albenga. She looked in at the garden as she passed the hotel. The strangers rose from a seat among the orange-trees and suddenly faced her. With a cry of fear she stood still, for one of them in astonishment darted towards her. It was Mrs. Oswell.

CHAPTER XVIII.

"MRS. BELCHER!" Mrs. Oswell darted from her husband's side through the little gateway and stopped in astonishment. Katherine stood spell-bound and helpless, the tears gathering in her eyes and her hands twisting nervously together as she vainly tried to speak. It was all over, she was discovered, and going to be taken back, a prisoner, to a judge who would be merciless. Then Mrs. Oswell, just as if she had divined her thoughts, put her arms round the girl's neck and kissed her. "Don't be afraid," she said. "I have understood all about it, and we are not going to telegraph to Mr. Belcher; so don't look at us as if we were dragons."

"It is all right, Mrs. Belcher," Mr. Oswell

said reassuringly ; "Bee and I were very sorry
for you, and felt that things must have been
pretty bad or you wouldn't have done it."

"Where is he?" Katherine asked in a
whisper.

"In England, I suppose," Mrs. Oswell
answered in a tone of distinct satisfaction.
"Let that comfort you.   But how did you get
here?   Everyone thought you were at the
bottom of the sea," she added cheerfully ;
"your trunk turned up from the wreck of an
American liner, and its owner was supposed to
be drowned."

"Its owner?" Katherine said, dazed, 'and
my trunk?   Oh, I remember, I gave it to a
chambermaid at Southampton!"

"Well, Mr. Belcher wears a hat-band for
you, and if you leave him alone I shouldn't be
surprised if some fine day he marries again."

"Oh! let him," Katherine cried, with a
great throb of relief, "and don't tell him that
you have found me.   I was never really married to him—I mean that it was never like

marriage," she added, in answer to the surprise on Mr. Oswald's face, "and we were miserable together. Let him live his life as he will, and let me go my own way."

"Are you alone, dear?" Mrs. Oswell asked in a low voice.

"Alone?" Katherine repeated, not even understanding the question. "Why, yes. I met an old friend on board ship and made friends with her people," the colour came to her face swiftly, "but they are not here. I am by myself at Laigueglia, and the only person I know is a poor woman dying at Alassio."

Mrs. Oswell put her arm through Katherine's. "Fred," she said to her husband, "let us take her into the hotel and make her dine with us; the bell will ring directly—she wants cheering up."

Almost before she was aware of it, they had carried their point, and Katherine found herself sitting with them in the *salle à manger* of the hotel. "And now, tell us what you have been doing with yourself all this time." Mrs.

Oswell's manner had not improved, though her face was as kindly as ever. "You look as if you had been standing still on one leg like the crane you once told me about."

"I have been journeying on in the world as I always longed to do," she said with a little rueful smile. "It is very beautiful, and the people in it have taught me to be very thankful for life; but I have known that an end must come. Oh, do tell me," she went on eagerly, and yet even to mention the name frightened her, "if you have seen—him. And what he said and whether he tried to find me?"

"We will tell you everything," Mrs. Oswell answered, "as soon as you have eaten some dinner. What a good thing this place is empty, so that we can talk in peace! Fred, do hurry the waiter. Oh, you have ordered some champagne—that was clever of you, it will do her good, even if it is bad. Let me see the label—I declare we are lucky! No, my dear Katherine, I have not seen Mr. Belcher, but

Fred has, two or three times. I have seen your aunt——"

"My aunt! I haven't one."

"Yes, you have," Mrs. Oswell answered triumphantly. "Your uncle went to Australia to look after his son's wife and two boys; and it seems that a Frenchwoman who lived in the same house in Gower Street insisted on going too."

"The artfulness of women is amazing," said Mr. Oswell.

"Only when they are French, Fred dear. Well, when they got to Melbourne it turned out that the boys were alive and the mother was dead. So your uncle married the French-woman, and they all came back together, and are living happy ever after."

"I can't imagine Uncle Robert married," Katherine said in amazement. "Mr. Belcher won't get his money."

"Serve him right."

"But how did you see her? You didn't know Uncle Robert."

"No, but Fred had met him at your house, and I was miserable about you, so I boldly called on her and told her freely my opinion of Mr. Belcher. She is a nice woman, and had admired you when you went to see your uncle. I am quite sure that she will be a friend to you."

"How did you know that I had run away?"

"I went to see you, and Gibson said you had gone to Bridgewater, and gave me the address, so I wrote to you there, and the letter was returned to your house. I believe that first set up your husband's suspicions on his return. He was in a great rage, and persisted in believing that a woman at Bridgewater——"

"Oh, poor Susan——"

"Was hiding you. He felt certain that you were there, for you had been traced to Paddington. A month or two later there was a sensational wreck, and among the things cast up was the box with your name——"

20

"Susan thought it would look nice, and had it painted on when I was married."

"So Mr. Belcher concluded that you were drowned, and," she added with the occasional want of tact which had always distinguished her, "I think he has quite done mourning for you by this time."

"It sets me free," Katherine said, with a long sigh of satisfaction ; "he shall never know that I am alive."

"Well, but—I don't think that would be quite fair," Mr. Oswell said. "Suppose some day he married again—you would have led him into bigamy. It is rather an unpleasant fix, I know," he went on, looking at her with the kind eyes that she remembered at Windermere, "but we have to get out of our awkward fixes in life with the best grace we can, and we must all play the game fairly. You and Bee had better talk it over presently. And in spite of all things," he added, as he filled up her glass, "we will drink to your happiness, Mrs. Belcher."

"Happiness! I never knew what happiness was—till this summer," and the colour rushed to her face again.

Mrs. Oswell watching her, thought sagely, "Unless I am very much mistaken, my dear, you have been in sight of the red lamp since you took to journeying about the world alone. A woman gravitates towards it as if by instinct when her home relations go wrong." Then she asked aloud, "What made you come to this place, of all others?"

"It was your talk at Windermere," Katherine answered, looking at Mr. Oswell. "I never dreamt that you would come again: Mrs. Oswell said she didn't like the little Italian places."

"It's very odd," Mrs. Oswell said affectionately, "but no matter how much I dislike them at first, I always come round to thinking that the things Fred likes and does are the best in the world. I positively longed to come abroad again, and made him bring me here, and now I am convinced that it is the loveliest place I ever saw. We are going away in the morning to Monte Carlo, but we mean to get home for Christmas—who would believe that it only wants a fortnight to it, in this lovely weather?"

"And you won't tell Mr. Belcher that you have seen me?" Katherine entreated.

"Did he treat you very badly?" Mr. Oswell asked.

"He made me miserable," she answered sadly. "The morning I came away, and the night before, he struck me—even to think of him frightens me." Mr. Oswell was silent a moment, then he answered slowly;

"You will have to let him know that you are alive, my dear young lady; it may be hard lines, but if there is a law one has to abide by it. We will take care of you," he went on gently, "and see that he doesn't ill-treat you. Perhaps he would consent to a legal separation; then, at least, you would not go about dreading discovery, only it seems hard that you should have no future before you but that of a woman separated from her husband—which is never a very satisfactory one."

"I did not dream what I was doing when I married," Katherine said despairingly.

"People never do, my dear," Mrs. Oswell said; "but still there you are. Fred wants to smoke, I know—he shall go and walk on the beach while you and I sit in the orange-garden and have a quiet talk; and presently we will take you back to Laigueglia. We start by the early train, so we shall not see you to-morrow. I can't think," she went on as they walked down the pathway, "how I could be so wicked to Fred as not to enjoy Italy the last time he brought me."

"Are you as happy together as ever?" Katherine asked.

"Happier."

"Were you very much in love when you married?"

"We liked each other better than anyone else, and wanted to be together; but things didn't always go smoothly the first year. I

have never owned that to anybody else in the
world," Mrs. Oswell added. "It was difficult
for him, perhaps, to settle down with a woman
always about him, to come home always to
the same face and the same sort of talk, and
to give up some of his bachelor habits—though
I am pretty easy-going—and of course I am
expensive, so that he has had to work harder,
and his responsibilities are greater because of
me."

"Yes; but he has had you to love him
and to think of him and welcome him home
every day, and to sympathise with him, and
to care for everything that concerned him."

"And he has cared for everything that concerned me," Mrs. Oswell answered. "The ad-
vantages of his position, my dear, I leave for
his contemplation; it is my business to consider the disadvantages, and to try and lighten
them. We have each put up with the other's
shortcomings and been thoroughly happy together. I certainly love him more than anyone else in the world—more and more as time

goes on—as he does me. But I suspect that
if we had not displayed some tact and forbear-
ance at times, especially in the beginning, we
could have drifted apart."

"Mrs. Oswell," asked Katherine slowly,
"are you saying this for me? Do you think
I ought to go back to Mr. Belcher?"

"I think you ought to let him know that
you are alive; and, if you are to fight, why,
fight fairly."

"He made me marry him, and he delighted
in making me miserable."

"Made or not made, you did marry him.
I always feel so sorry for the disagreeable
people myself; they have generally had some
knocks in life of which we know nothing; but
I remember saying this to you at Windermere.
If things had always gone well and smoothly
with Mr. Belcher, he would probably have
been kinder and more gentle with you. We
pass on all things to each other."

"That is what I once thought about sin,"
Katherine exclaimed.

"I think," Mrs. Oswell went on, not heeding her, "that we should always try, as a modern thinker said he tried, 'to accept the facts as they are, however bitter or severe, to be a lover and a student but never a lawgiver.'"

"It is so hard," Katherine whispered; "and Mr. Belcher need never even see me again."

"I know it is hard," Mrs. Oswell answered; "but try and consider things from his point of view. It won't be pleasant for him to have a discontented wife all his days, or even to go about with an invisible millstone round his neck, while you become that most disagreeable invention of modern times, a lone woman with a husband, a past, and a grievance."

"What do you want me to do?" she asked slowly.

"Write to your uncle and ask him to try and improve matters; and, if they can't be improved, why, of course, you must arrange a separation. Have courage, dear; we will stand by you, and I think your uncle's wife will be a good friend to you."

"Oh, Mrs. Oswell!" Katherine cried passionately, resting her head down on the back of the seat, "I cannot do it, I cannot. It isn't only that I don't care for him—I hate him and shrink from him. He is horrible—horrible! even to think of him makes me shudder. There cannot be anything in the world so cruel as to be married to a man you don't love; and it isn't only that I don't love him," she added desperately, "but that I love somebody else. You have been very kind to me, and so I will tell you all. I love somebody else with all my heart and soul, and think of him every minute of my life, and long to be with him, and every day away from him—and all my days must be spent away from him—is an ache and a sorrow. He is not here, and I shall never see him again."

"Thank God!" Mrs. Oswell said to herself.

"In a little more than a month he will have started for India, and I shall never, never see him again," repeated poor Katherine woefully. "But he loved me—he loved me so, and he wanted to marry me. Oh! Mrs. Oswell, I should have been the happiest woman in the world."

"But didn't he know that you were married?" Suddenly Mrs. Oswell looked down at Katherine's fingers: "Why, where is your wedding-ring?"

"I threw it into the sea," she answered, with a satisfaction she could not help. "No, he didn't know; he thought I was a girl."

"But does he know now?" Mrs. Oswell was a little shocked and bewildered, easy-going though she was by nature.

"Yes, yes; he knows everything, and probably despises me and thinks me even worse than you do, for he and his mother—they were together, and I stayed with them at Generoso —could not understand why I refused him, though I loved him and made no secret of it, till I stood up one night and told them the truth. But I could not bring myself to tell them that he had struck me. It seemed ungenerous to tell that of a man they had never seen, and who was not there to defend himself. Besides, my pride would not let me confess it, it was so humiliating, and when I had finished, almost before they had had time to recover, I vanished from their sight, and the next morning I got up very early and left a note for Miss Bennett—she was to be carried down in a chair from Generoso and did not want me till she reached Mendrisio. I started on foot at five in the morning. It was chilly and raining," she went on with a shudder, "though afterwards I saw the sun shining up on the mountains. I shall never forget that long walk down while I live—it was like walking down from Heaven. Miss Bennett followed earlier than I expected, and we got away by the morning train, perhaps before they even found out that we had started. I wrote to Mrs. Alford from here, but her answer showed that she was angry with me, and Jim didn't send me a single word. All that is over, Mrs. Oswell, but I love him with all my heart, and could be happy with him, though we were beggars in the street and he beat me every day. That is the whole difference. How could I go back to Mr. Belcher, and be a wife to him whom I never loved at all—never did anything but fear —while in my heart I am always with another man and belong to him?"

"Well," said Mrs. Oswell, with a long sigh, "it is a terrible corner, and I don't see what is to be done."

"Leave me alone," Katherine entreated, "and tell no one that you have seen me. You shall hear from me later—after I have seen poor Miss Bennett die, perhaps. Leave me alone —wait—wait till I have thought it all out for myself and write to you. I want to do what is right, I do indeed, but some things are not to be borne."

"There is no merit in doing right when it is easy; it is the difficulty that makes it virtue."

"And even then it is only duty. Oh, Mrs. Oswell, I have come to the conclusion that morality is often the sorriest thing in the world. But I am not a foolish girl any longer. I am a woman who has suffered and thought, and loved and striven, and I want to do my best—my very, very best—but I must fight it out alone; I must be alone to work out my own salvation or the reverse. Remember," she added with a sob, "whichever it is—it will be mine, mine to bear, for ever and ever." She stopped, but her face was on her arm, which was twisted over the back of the seat. Mrs. Oswell looked at her puzzled; these strong emotions did not often come her way, and she did not know what to do with them.

"Don't be so unhappy," she said. "Things may turn out better than we imagine, and, of course, though it may seem rather hard now, it is a good thing that the other man is going to India, for, after all, we women are very human, my dear. I wish you would talk it out with Fred—there is nothing like a mascu-

line head for leavening two feminine ones, and
he liked you from the first. I feel sure it would
do you good if you talked it over with him,
dear."

"I can't talk it over with anyone any more,"
Katherine answered desperately. "Let me go
back to Laigueglia. I am glad to have seen
you both. You have been very good to me,
and I know you will be, but let me be for a
little while, and then I will write to you; and
till then promise not to say that you have seen
me."

"Yes, dear, I will, we both will."

"Now let me go."

"Are you in a pension?"

"No, I have a room over a little shop in
Laigueglia. It looks on the sea. I want to go
back and sit in the dark and think it all out
by myself."

They walked back with her almost in
silence, along the bare white road, beside the
sea. The village was dark and still, though it
was hardly eight o'clock, for light is dear in

Italy, and the little lamp beside which the peasants sit on the long winter evenings hardly do more than betray the shadows round them. The church at the end of the little street looked high and staring white ; the sands and the dark sea beyond were plain enough, but they could make out nothing else. They stopped before the house in which Katherine lodged ; the shop was closed, there was no sign or sound of life ; but she pushed open the door and showed them that it had been left ajar in order to admit her. Mrs. Oswell looked curiously in at the narrow passage, but there was nothing to be seen. For one moment Katherine thought of asking her to enter and see the room that was now her home, but her courage failed, she wanted to be alone so much. She was aching to get up to it—the little whitewashed room with the coloured pictures round it, and the fantastic ceiling decorated in cheap Italian fashion—she wanted to throw open the window and look outwards towards the sea.

"Good-bye," and she held out her hands. Mrs. Oswell kissed her on both cheeks.

"You must write to us," she said.

"After the New Year," Katherine answered, putting her weary head down for one moment on the friendly shoulder; "I want to rest and be still till then."

"It will be the best thing for you," Mr. Oswell said understandingly, "and be assured that we shall say nothing till you give us leave."

CHAPTER XIX.

She groped her way up-stairs and pushed open the door. The room was faint with the scent of flowers she had gathered in the morning. She struck a match and looked round as if to be sure that the place was the same one, and she the same woman who had come back to it after the experiences of the evening. A white letter on the table caught her eye; it had come by hand and not by post. "Jim!" she cried. "A letter from Jim!" and she clutched it in her left hand, while with the right she tremblingly held the match to a candle. Then she tore open the envelope.

"*We are on our way to England, and I stopped at Alassio, in order to see you. Am going on by the next train,* 10.20 *to-night.*

21   (319)

Miss Bennett said you had left her to return to
your place, but there seems to be some mistake.
I will get food, and return at a little before
nine, and walk as far as the church and back.
If you get this, will you let me see you, even
if it is only for a minute ? "

"And I might have missed you," she
gasped. "Oh, my dear ! To think I shall see
you again ! " She read his letter a second
time, and kissed it ; then joyfully extinguished
the light and went down the dark stairs, out of
the house and swiftly along the street, feeling
like a swallow flying south. Someone was
waiting by the church. She stopped and hesitated, and a little cry escaped her.

"Oh, Jim, dear—oh, Jim ! I thought I
should never, never see you again. I can't
bear it—I can't bear it, indeed. The happiness
is too great"—and she burst into tears.

"Why, Kathy—my dear Kathy." He put
his arms round her, and looked down at her
face, though in the dim light he could hardly
see it. "Is it as bad as that, my dear? I

hoped that it was better for you, and that it was only I who went on caring. I couldn't make myself go away for ever without seeing you once more, or without a single word——"

"Oh, Jim!" she whispered with a great sigh of thankfulness. "I thought we should never meet again. Nothing in the world will matter now."

"My poor little girl—look here—let us come and sit on the beach. I saw a seat there. The population of Laigueglia appears to be dead and buried."

"Oh, to think that we are together again, and by the Mediterranean," she said in a voice trembling with joy. "It is like a wonderful dream." And she clung to his arm as they went towards the sea. "Now, tell me," she went on, when they had found the seat—"tell me, have you been angry—what did you think —why didn't you send me a single word in the Mummy's letter?"

"Angry, my child? No. I have thought nothing except that I love you, and for that

reason had better not write. I was ill when
the Mummy wrote—that confounded fever got
hold of me again—but we thought that it
would worry you if you knew. I say, what a
wonderful place this is! I wish we could stay
here for ever, you and I." He looked up for
a moment as a breath from the orange-trees
was wafted to him. To the left was the still
village, to the right the Corniche road going
on to Andora; in front the sands and the sea;
a little way ahead, at each end of the bay,
were the dark rocks, and on the left the island
of Gallinara; in the background were the
mountains, and over everything the strange
spell of night and silence. "If we could only
have a century of it," he said, with a long sigh.

"Ah, if we could," she echoed eagerly.
"But tell me about the Mummy—where is
she?"

"At present she is waiting for me at Ven-
timiglia. We came from Genoa to-day, get to
England the day after to-morrow. I told her
I must see you again; the train goes by the

station, and I couldn't pass it. She was very angry, and thought it wrong; perhaps it is, but never mind. I got out at Alassio as we came by, and go on by the next train, 10.20, which is the mail through to Marseilles. We should have had to wait for it in any case, and I wait here with you."

"And she wouldn't come and see me too?" He shook his head. "And she won't forgive me?"

"My dear, she wants you to write to your uncle, or else to go to England as soon as I am gone, to her house, and to let her write to your husband and see what can be done."

"And do you wish it too?"

"I can't wish it," he said gently, "but something ought to be done."

"He thinks that I am dead," and she explained briefly the mistake about her box and the meeting with the Oswells. "Why should he ever know that I am alive? Jim, I have been sorry that I told you," she whispered. "You might have married me and taken me to India and nobody would have known. He would have been thankful that I was dead, and we should have been happy all our lives. It would have done no one any harm. I couldn't have done it because I couldn't have borne to deceive you. But would it have been wrong?"

"It doesn't do to fly in the face of the law; it has a way of avenging itself."

"Yes, I know—Mr. Oswell said that too; but would it have been wrong in itself? Would it be wrong if you took me away now and he never knew that I was alive, and we were faithful to each other all our lives?"

"It won't do, dear," and he shook his head. "We have got to do the best we can in the world and to put the best we know into it."

"But it wouldn't do anyone any harm," she pleaded.

"That is a thing we can never insure. Look here, Kathy," he said, resting his two hands across her shoulder and trying to see her face through the darkness. "Suppose we did as you say, and called each other man and wife in India."

"I always feel as if I were married to you," she whispered.

"Do you, my sweet? Tell me why."

"Because we loved each other and told each other so, up at Generoso. And you kissed me," she whispered, lower still, but with a courage the darkness gave her, "and held me in your arms, and I knew that you cared for me, and I felt my heart so full of love for you. Nothing can undo it, nothing as long as I live, or try as much as I will—it is like a marriage tie."

"And it shall be like one to me," he said tenderly; "but we are going to do the right thing for all that, and not the wrong one. Suppose, as I say, my darling, that we did live as man and wife in India, and he found it out. There would be a divorce."

"But that would set me free."

"At a terrible price. We might have children some day, you and I; we should wish for

them if we were natural people. Would you
like them to grow up and find out our dis-
grace? It is no good, my dear, nothing will
make a wrong thing right, and no amount of
repenting will ever undo it. We should have
to turn the world backwards to blot it out,
even though we were forgiven a dozen times
over, for a deed once done is done to all eternity, that is what we so seldom realise. I
love you with all my heart, God knows; but
I am not going to make the woman I love
afraid to look other people in the face. The
fact that we love each other ought to make
us strong enough to do the right thing, or the
love is rather poor stuff. The hardness of it
won't be all yours; it will be worse for me in
India, knowing that you are with him, perhaps, and with an indefinite dread that will
make me long to blow his brains out."

"Oh, Jim, I know that you are right,"
and resting her face down on his hands she
kissed them. "Yes, let me," she said, as he
tried to draw them away. "Let me, I want

to kiss your hands, I am not good enough for you to kiss my face—for I have been trying to make you do wrong."

"No, she hasn't," he said tenderly, "she is only a little weak woman—my little Eve, and I love her, my dear, my sweet, I love her. And since she can't be my wife, I will promise her never to marry anyone else as long as I live."

"But I should like you to marry and be happy, Jim. When you say that you love me it makes me feel as if I could do anything in the wide world," and she took his hands and put them together, and rested her forehead down upon them. "Anything in the wide world," she repeated, after a long minute's silence, "no matter how difficult it is. It gives me strength, and I will prove it—I will, indeed. Give me a little time just to gather myself together, and you shall see. Don't ask me—I can't tell you, but it shall be done—not yet, but in a little time. When do you start for India?"

"On the 26th of January."

"Till then," she said with a gasp. "Till that day let your poor Eve live in her Eden, to think of you and love you, and grow strong to do that which is most difficult. Hark! the clocks are striking. Those are the Alassio clocks; we hear them all this way when the wind is in the right quarter. What time does your train go, Jim? Ten-twenty? That was half-past nine," she went on excitedly. "You must go, dearest, you must go, and perhaps it is better. Let me walk back with you to Alassio; the late train doesn't stop here. Let us have this one last walk together."

"No. You would have to come back alone and in the dark. I shall scurry along quickly enough by myself. We will have five minutes more together here, my sweet, and then good-bye."

"Shall you write to me?" she asked.

"Better not. We shall hear of each other through the Mummy. All things have to be paid for, Kathy. Is even the sorrow of parting too big a price for having met and loved each other?"

"No," she whispered, "and I will make it another-thank offering, Jim, dear, be sure of that, though to-night I can't tell you how or when it will be."

"It is time to go," he said reluctantly, and turned her face up to his and looked at it as though he never expected to see it again in this world. Then they walked back slowly to the village.

"Jim," she said, "you will go past Laigueglia in the train. I will listen for it by the open window, and shall see it as it goes by between me and the sea."

"I sha'n't know which is your window."

"Yes, you shall," she exclaimed. "I will light a candle and hold it up, and you will see it in the darkness and know when you are passing me."

"That is splendid, my darling. By Jove! I have a box of lights in my pocket; I will

light one as an answer. You will see it plainly. What! is this the place already?"

"Yes, Jim, already," she answered woefully.

A quarter past ten. She was standing by
the open window counting the minutes: five
more and he would start from Alassio. "I will
do it," she was saying to herself. "Oh, my
dear, my dear, what does the rest matter now
that I have had that one hour with you, have
seen your face and heard your voice and felt
your kisses? I could walk to the stake and be
burnt and not feel it while this joy is so strong
upon me. It helps me to know how they bore
things in the old days for love of Christ. Oh,
Jim, my dear, my dear! There is nothing I
would not do for love of you. Hark! it is
coming—the train has started—he will be here
directly!" With feverish haste she lighted
the candle and stood with it by the open window looking out into the darkness. Nearer
and nearer it rumbled—nearer—quicker—it
was passing. She waved the flickering can-

dle, and suddenly there was a little flash from one of the windows of the dark train. A cry escaped her: "Oh, my darling!" she exclaimed. "It is all over for ever and ever; but I will do even that for love of you!"

CHAPTER XX.

THE weeks dragged by. Every day lagged, every hour drew itself out to the uttermost, and yet each one as it passed left dread and fright wrapped closer and closer round Katherine's heart. She felt as if she were living her last days of life ; in three weeks the end would come, and she knew perfectly what that end would be. Sometimes the old longing beset her to journey on and see the rest of the world. "My dear beautiful world," she said to herself as she walked up the little red road towards the spot where King Otho's daughter had once lived in a cottage and found happiness, "I wish I could go on—could tramp on through you for ever, seeing all your seas, looking up at your mountains, and staying to rest a little among the people who belong to you. I am strong and well and young, and don't want to die; but when I do I am glad to think that I shall be put into the earth and grow into it till I become just a little part of the world itself. Perhaps some day I shall come out in the sunshine again, and feel it falling soft and warm upon me; or shall have seed planted in me and flowers growing up, or wind myself round the root of a great tree while my soul climbs into a branch and looks down on the little figures walking to and fro, till it is time for them, too, to pay themselves as tribute into the earth on which they have lived."

The New Year came. Miss Bennett was dying, painlessly, but surely. Her sister had arrived, a gaunt, cheerful woman, evidently quite reconciled to her sister's going, and hoping not to be detained too long away from her husband and children.

"Poor Sarah was a woman who always grumbled," she explained to Katherine—it was the last afternoon of Miss Bennett's life. "She was never satisfied with things, and I don't wonder; she found them pretty hard, poor dear. Father wasn't fond of her as a child, and after mother died he hurried her away from home to earn her living. She taught French and music in schools for years, and saved a little money, and went to stay with some rich cousins in Staffordshire; and that was the worst thing that ever happened to her, for she fell in love with a man who has been the ruin of her life, though she hasn't seen him for years and years now."

"How was he the ruin of her life?" Katherine asked. She and Mrs. Wells were walking up and down the garden of the pension, while Miss Crockett watched a few minutes beside the invalid.

"He thought she was well off, so he made love to her, and she liked him. Afterwards, when he found she had no money, he jeered at the idea of marriage, and deserted her. She has never ceased thinking of him, or cared for anyone else, though she knows perfectly what he is.   It is knowing what he is that has made her so hard and dissatisfied."

"But do you think she likes him still?"

"I feel certain that she thinks of him day and night, though she hasn't seen him for fifteen years.   He's a bad man, and cares for nothing but money and hurting people who come in his way.   Some men like to see others suffer, and he does ; for I know many things about him besides his conduct to Sarah.   I saw him just before I left London, and told him she was dying.   He said she had written and asked him to come out and say good-bye to her."

"And he refused?"

"He was too busy, he said, and a cruel, triumphant look came over his face, as if he rejoiced that she was dying and alone.   I don't wonder his wife ran away from him, though he only married her a year or two ago—a girl, too, as if any girl would live with Edward Belcher!"

"Edward Belcher!   Is that his name?"

22

Katherine exclaimed. Mrs. Wells was looking at the orange-trees, and did not see her face.

"Yes, that is his name," she answered. "And Sarah has spent her whole life loving a man who doesn't even exist, or, rather, wasted it, hoping he would be different and begin to exist as she imagined him, and that he, who has never cared for anything or anyone but himself, would then begin to care for her. Well, I have a good husband myself, and I don't believe in men being bad, unless it is one now and then, but I don't believe that men ever suffer what women do on their account; it is a good thing if some of us can plague them a bit. Let's go in. Miss Crockett said she would put up a white handkerchief at the window when Sarah woke, and I saw her pin it to the curtain."

Miss Bennett was awake and sensible. Her eyes wandered restlessly round the room. "I don't want you, Grace," she said to her sister; "I want to talk to Katherine about her own concerns, while you go and get her some tea. I have been thinking about that money," she said when they were alone—"the hundred pounds that came to Generoso. Did you send it to me? You wanted to give me some money a few days before. I thought, perhaps——" She closed her eyes for a moment, unable to go on. "Did you?" she asked, clutching at the frill of the square white pillow under her head.

"No, indeed, I didn't," Katherine answered; and wondered whether she might tell her the truth. But while she hesitated, a smile that was almost happy broke over Miss Bennett's face.

"I am glad of that," she said, "and Grace knows nothing about it either. I think," and she looked up with a strange expression in her eyes, "that it was sent me by someone I have known a long, long time, and used to like very much. I am glad he sent it," she whispered; "it shows that he thought of me, and wanted me to be comfortable at the last. I wish you knew him, Katherine; perhaps you will one day. I heard only lately that he married someone who was called Kerr. Perhaps it was a relation—you will know him," she went on in a half-rambling manner, "then you can give him the message. Grace never liked him, and perhaps she wouldn't give it."

"Give what message?" Katherine asked, in a low voice.

"To Edward. I should like him to know that nothing made any difference—perhaps he didn't mean to be unkind. He had to be prudent—a man has to be prudent, you know. Perhaps things were hard upon him when he was a boy—it always tells oh people when they grow up."

"What shall I say to him?"

"That I sent him my love. I know you will do it some day, for you are a good girl, and I hope you will marry young Alford. Don't let anything stand in the way—it is a pity to let anything stand in the way—money or anything." She shut her eyes for a moment, and then the smile broke over her face again. "I am glad that I know," she said, in a happy satisfied voice, "that he sent me his money—he has given me everything I have had for the last two months—he must have felt that I belonged to him."

That night Miss Bennett died.

CHAPTER XXI.

ANOTHER fortnight, nearly three weeks, and then Katherine sat in her little room at Laigueglia writing letters. She felt as if she would never get through them, for she stopped so many times to gather courage: every word seemed to be torn out of her heart and life. The first one was to Mrs. Alford.

"Jim told me that you were very angry," it ran, "and I could tell that it was so from the letter you sent me before he came. But you said in that letter, and he repeated it, that you wished me to go to you if I did what you and he considered to be right. And this I am going to do, dear Mummy. I know Jim starts on the twenty-sixth, a week to-morrow,

and on that day I shall leave Laigueglia and
journey slowly towards England,—slowly, for
my feet will have to be dragged one after the
other even though they are taking me to you
at Chilworth. I will write to my uncle by
this post, as you wished, telling him everything that I have done, and giving him your
address, and saying that he will find me there.
I will write to Mr. Belcher too, telling him
that I am coming, and that Uncle Robert will
know my whereabouts. Now, will you forgive
me everything, dearest Mummy? Though I
fear I do not do it so much for love of what is
right, as for love of Jim and you. But just as
I have learnt to see that of one sin another is
born, so perhaps of one good deed, and that your
kindness to me, and of one thing that is divine
—for surely love that is strong and pure is divine—good may be born! However terrible it is
to do, I know that what I am doing is right—
though it seems to me as if the wrong would
have been better, since it would have made for
happiness. But this, again, is only one of the

342 A FLASH OF SUMMER.

tangles we cannot understand, and I know that we should steer towards the light, though we lose everything we care for most on the way. I know, too, that I would give thankfully and joyfully any hopes or happiness that might be mine, or even my life itself, for love of Jim and you, and I give you this deed in token of it.

"I shall be with you on Monday night, dear Mummy, and will tell Uncle Robert so. Perhaps he will not come to me till Tuesday, and then I shall have that little time alone with you, and you will make me strong to carry out all this; and I will love you and try to comfort you a little because Jim is with you no longer. Let me send my love to him—for love of him has only led me to do what is right, dear Mummy, and I do not think that Heaven would grudge it to me. Tell him that I shall start on my journey towards you on that same day—Friday, the 26th—that he will start on his away from you.

"Your loving KATHERINE."

Then there came the long explanatory letter to her Uncle Robert, and one to Mrs. Oswell telling her all that she had done and beg-
ging that she might find a line awaiting her
when she arrived at Chilworth. And then she
wrote a little note to Susan, apologising for all
the trouble she had caused her, and hoping that some day they might meet again.
Last of all there was the letter to her husband. It was more difficult than any other to
write:

". . . You never cared for me," she said,
"but I do not wonder, for I was so much
younger than you, and knew so little; I always felt in your way—and I was. But I was
not fair to you, and did wrong when I took my
fate altogether into my own hands, and I beg
you to forgive me and to let me live quietly
away from you, so that you do not remember
anything about me to vex you. It is no use
pretending that I care for you or could be
happy with you, for that would be untrue;
but I will leave everything in Uncle Robert's

hands ; he will tell you where I am and decide what is best to be done."

She went out while her strength lasted and posted her letters, feeling as if they held her death-sentence, and she were going to follow them to the place of execution. She walked back along the sands and picked up a Venus's slipper, and having looked at it wonderingly threw it into the sea. She remembered the orange garden behind the hotel, and went back towards it, and up a mountain pathway for half a mile and looked round at the sea and the bay and the island, and the mountain chain right and left of her : soon she would have seen it all for the last time. She gathered some Banxia roses, and went up higher. There was a little ruined chapel dedicated to the Virgin. She sat down and leant her head against its wall. " She was a woman and suffered, and it comforts me to sit here," she said to herself. "If only I could understand things better ! Why should so many women have prayed and wept out their hearts to the Virgin if she cannot hear or help them ; and if she can, why is the knowledge of it denied to so many others? It seems sometimes as if we were all hopelessly blind and deaf, or as if there were some strange senses in us tied down and unable to explain the things that are or are not. It isn't to be wondered at if most of us go astray. If I wanted to make myself more miserable still, it would be easy enough to sit and think that love and pain and death and the wide world's beauty are the only things that really exist."

Friday morning — the twenty - sixth — dawned.

She was going to leave Laigueglia by the ten o'clock train. Jim would not start from Chilworth till the afternoon, for she remembered hearing him say that the Indian mail started late. She had never travelled very far alone by land before, but what did it matter? Suppose she were killed, it would not be worse than going back to Mr. Belcher. She had miscalculated the time the journey would take when she wrote her letters. She might have stayed at Laigueglia till Saturday night or Sunday morning, and yet been in time to get to.Mrs. Alford's by Monday night; but having said that she would start on Friday, she could not bring herself to depart from a word that she had written. So she stood packed and ready at the little station. The Italian woman with whom she had lodged came to see her off, and kissed her, and gave her a bough of oranges as a parting gift, and Katherine thought her heart would break when she heard her last "Addio, Signora!" as the train moved off. She saw her own little window from the train—the window to which she had held up the light as Jim went by with an answering flash. But she tried to keep down all thoughts of him and of that night by the sea. It must be forgotten; everything must be forgotten, except that for his sake—his sake, and not the Mummy's, as her heart knew well—she was going to do this saddest, hardest thing on earth.

The train went on in the sunshine between the mountains, and the landscape yellow with oranges on the one hand, and the blue sea on the other. She looked from side to side wonderingly, and it seemed as if every moment the earth grew more beautiful, but she was going away from it. Past all the little villages with the happy peasants in them, and the shrines and the churches and the little town with the prison in the shape of a cross; past San Remo, with its big hotels and air of fashion; past Bordighera with its palm-trees, and on to Ventimiglia; then, like a dream-woman, she got out to change over to the French side, wondering if it could be really true that she was awake, taking this journey alone, and in order to give herself up to Mr. Belcher.

All manner of wild ideas came into her head as she scurried along. She thought of Eltham Palace and the moat, and the crane standing on one leg. Perhaps it remembered Anne Boleyn, and knew how she felt on her way to Tower Hill. She thought of Alice

Alford's joke about Anne dancing with her head in her pocket in the palace of Eltham. There was a gallery at one end in which the musicians had sat, never dreaming that perhaps some day their ghosts would come back and sit there playing music that had no sound in it, to an empty hall turned into a barn. Katherine felt as if she were going through life with her head in her pocket. Who knows? She might dance or laugh—what did it matter? All the time she would be a dead woman. And then she laughed out bitterly, and broke down and cried, and told herself for the thousandth time that nothing would matter more, her life had come to an end, and she was going back to Mr. Belcher for an eternity. She slept at Marseilles, a long dreamless sleep, a stranger in a strange land and a big hotel, and wondered in the morning what to do next, for she had too much time on her hands. It would have been far better to rush the journey through. Finally, she decided to stay all day at Marseilles ; but she had no heart to walk about. She was a prisoner going back to gaol, and had no business to behave like a free woman.

So Saturday passed. Jim was in the train; she was not sure of his route, but she imagined that he must be somewhere in the middle of France. It was something to be in the same land with him. "Good-bye," she said to herself; "I am doing this for you, and you know it by this time. Good-bye." She left Marseilles that night, and travelled through to Paris, and stayed another long day in an hotel seeing nothing of the city to which she had come. What a strange thing it was to be there and not to move a step outward! But she was a prisoner, she told herself again, and had no more right than she had heart to go a-pleasuring. She meant to start at night again—it seemed easier to travel in the dark, for then she could not see the distance lessening between her and her doom. But on the way to Calais she shook off her depression, and felt her courage come back. After all, Mr. Belcher

was certain to consent to a separation. Had
he not told her that he liked somebody else
better? Oh, how terrible it was to remember
that, and to think of poor Miss Bennett dying
happily because she imagined that Jim's
money had come from the man who had
ruined her life! It was this last knowledge
that added a touch of horror to her thoughts
of Mr. Belcher. But Miss Bennett was at rest,
poor soul; and as for her—for Katherine—she
felt that Uncle Robert would manage things,
and would not be so cruel as to let her go back
to jeers and blows; and now that there was
probably no prospect of any money Mr. Belcher would not desire it.

She reached Charing Cross in the early
morning, and still her courage held by her.
After all, she was going to the Mummy that
day, to see Jim's home, to hear how he had set
forth, and whether he had left a message for
her; perhaps he had written her just a word
to wish her a last good-bye. But there was
another long day to get through first. She

felt shy of going to Chilworth before the evening ; the Mummy would not expect her, and
might have other visitors. Then suddenly the
idea struck her that she would go to Eltham ;
the crane was gone long years ago ; but there
was the palace and the moat, and the way
through the church and across the corn-field to
the woods that led to Shooter's Hill.

So she walked through the quaint old place
that day and stood before the palace, and saw
the moat, and the little bridge and the gnarled
trees, that looked as if centuries had passed
since they were saplings. Then she went on to
the church ; and suddenly the bells rang out
a peal. Two people were being married ; she
wondered if they loved each other, and
whether they thought it all a joke, and marriage a pastime that did not need much thinking about before they entered upon it, and,
above all, if they were taking each other of
their own free will or because they had been
talked and persuaded into it. She went across
the corn-fields, brown and bare in the winter

23

sunshine, and over the stile to the woods. A
wooden hoarding had been put up on one
side of them : someone had enclosed half the
ground. What did it matter? Perhaps she
would never see them again. She trod the
dead leaves under foot, and looked up through
the brown boughs and twigs at the winter sky.
There were hips and blackberry briars trailing
on either side the pathway with scarce a leaf
upon them ; but the holly-bushes looked green
and sturdy. A thrush flew overhead, giving
out a sweet, fresh note, and a little robin
hopped along the ground as though it were a
bird of lowlier degree. She sat down on a tree
that had been felled, and spent a whole two
hours thinking : then a clock in the distance
struck two. It was time to go. She was afraid
to walk round by Severndroog Tower, for it
was there that Mr. Belcher had found her on
the evening that he asked her to marry him.
She took the narrow path that led to the high
road opposite the Bull, and walked slowly down
Shooter's Hill till she came to the turning with

the well at the corner. The White House was only a step beyond. A high fence, through which she could not see, half hid it from the roadway ; but the strangers who had come to live there had children, for she heard their voices playing in the garden. She turned back and went swiftly past the post-office and the Red Lion, till she came to the lane between the stuffed-bird shop and Ordnance Terrace— an old lady in a widow's cap, and a girl stood by the window of the first house. She thought of them for a minute as she hurried round the corner. She almost ran past the cottages in the lane and on to the common, and through the White Gate, and safely to the station.

It was more than an hour's journey from Charing Cross to Chilworth, and the twilight deepened into darkness as the train went through the pine woods of Surrey ; but she was there at last, and stood in the darkness and cold wondering what to do. She had a vague hope that there might be a message for her at the station, with some direction to the house, but there was none. The way was up a lane between two green hedges—the railway porter pointed it out—she could scarcely see it through the darkness. She walked on, afraid of the loneliness and stillness, for half a mile perhaps, then the road ascended, and she could dimly see that there was an open space with a road turning to the right and left.

"Mrs. Alford's," a man said in answer to her inquiry; "take the road to the left—it is the second house. You'll find 'Rooks' Nest' written up on the gate." Tired and footsore with the long day's tramp, but with a sense of scare and hurry that carried her along, she went for another quarter of a mile, then she stopped suddenly by a gate. It led to a house with fir-trees standing up black and straight beside it. She pushed open the gate and found her way to the door.

The bell rang loudly, as though the house inside were hollow. She could hardly keep her trembling self upright while she heard someone within coming to answer it. A tall woman of five-and-forty stood and looked at her. By the dim light of the hall Katherine could see that she was pale and sorrowful-looking.

"Is this Mrs. Alford's?" she asked in a voice she tried to make steady.

"Yes," said the woman slowly. "You are the lady from Italy, I suppose? I am to let you in—the mistress will see you for a minute. Will you come into the dining-room?" She led the way into a dark cold room, putting a light she carried from the hall down on the table. Then she shut the door and went towards Katherine and looked at her. "The mistress said I was to tell you first, ma'am, and before you went to her," she said with infinite pity in her voice. "You needn't mind my telling you instead of her, for I have been with them more or less these five-and-twenty years, and knew Mr. Jim since he was a little boy."

"Yes," said Katherine, not dreaming of what was to come.

"And the mistress told me how fond

you were of him and what a blow it would
be——"

"Yes, but what?" she asked, a dread of
something terrible taking hold of her. "Has
anything happened?"

"Yes," said the woman, nodding and speaking in a voice that was almost a sob, "the very
worst that could be has happened. Mr. Jim
was to start on Friday——"

"I know."

"And on Thursday night he died, dear
heart, and this day he was buried."

"Oh, my God!" Katherine cried, and fell
forward. But the woman caught her and
almost carried her to the leather sofa behind
them, and sat down beside her, and took off
her hat and smoothed the hair from her forehead. "Oh, no, no!" she said presently "it
can't be—it can't be!"

"Ah, poor dear, the mistress said you loved
him," the woman answered, "and what it
would be to you. It was the fever that took
him, on the top of a chill that he got just three

days before, and he seemed to have no strength to fight it off, though he had always been a strong man, and was, to look at, till the last."

Then a quarter of an hour went by, that in looking back upon afterwards always seemed to Katherine to have been like years.

"Did you say that she would see me?" she asked at last.

"Yes, ma'am, she will see you," the woman answered gently, with the helpful manner that only belongs to an old servant, "but you mustn't stay with her many minutes, for she has gone through a terrible day, and the doctor says she is better alone. But you shall see her, and then you must come away with me, and I'll give you food and put you to rest, and you shall cry your heart out, dear, for tears will help you most." Something in the woman's manner told Katherine that she knew the whole history of her coming. "There is a letter for you," she went on, "but you had better see the mistress first, and I'll get it for you meanwhile."

"Is it from Jim?" she asked, starting.

"No, it only came to-day."

Mrs. Alford was sitting in her own room in a high-backed easy chair, over a deadened fire. She turned her head, but made no other sign till Katherine, kneeling down in front of her, kissed her black dress. Then she lifted her hands and put them on the girl's head and folded her to her heart for a moment.

"He saw your letter," she said, "and told me to take care of you, dear. But I can't speak of it to-night, or think of any one but him."

"Oh, Mummy, dear Mummy!" came like a little wail from Katherine's lips, and there was a long silence.

"You shall belong to me," the old lady said again; "but you must leave me alone now. I am trying to think that it was a blessed thing to have had him to love, but it is hard to feel anything except that he has gone. You must go to Elizabeth." Then Katherine kissed her dress again, and the thin hands that rested on it, and went reverently from the room.

Elizabeth was waiting outside ; she had a letter in her hand and a lighted candle. "Perhaps you would like to read it," she said, and held up the light as they stood on the staircase. It was from Mrs. Oswell.

"*My dear*," it said, "*I have seen your aunt, and she has confided to me that your uncle has given Mr. Belcher your address— from a sense of duty, I suppose. Duty has many cruel things in this world to answer for. I let you know at once in case he should be down upon you, but remember Fred and I will stand by you hard and fast.*"

Katherine read it twice, but even then she was so dazed she could hardly take it in ; and when she did it seemed so trifling a calamity she could not realise it. She looked up at Elizabeth bewildered. "Which was his room ? " she asked, like a woman who was dreaming.

"That one just a few steps down," the woman answered, "there—above the hall. You had better not see it to-night, dearie."

"Yes, let me," she pleaded. Without a word Elizabeth led the way and opened the door. Stillness and death seemed to stare them in the face. There was a bookcase beside the fireplace, and on the other side were two portmanteaus and a tin case piled one on the other. Between the windows and the fireplace was a bedstead, but only a mattress covered with a sheet was on it, and at the head a pillow. Between the bed and the windows a space seemed to have been cleared; it looked as though something had stood there that had been carried out.

"Did he die there?" she asked, looking towards the bed.

"Yes," nodded Elizabeth; "with his head on that pillow. It may be you would like to be alone a few minutes," and putting the light on a chest of drawers, she went softly from the room. Then Katherine went up to the bed, and knelt down, took the pillow and hid her face in it.

Suddenly there was a sharp ringing of the front-door bell. She heard footsteps go towards it, and buried her face deeper into the pillow and pulled it round her head, and bit its white cover, and kissed it with the wild kisses of passion that only means despair. Then the door was opened, and her own name and a voice she knew well enough fell upon her ear. Someone entered, and the street-door was closed.

Mr. Belcher had found her.

THE END.

A JOURNEY IN OTHER WORLDS. A Romance of the Future. By JOHN JACOB ASTOR. With 9 full-page Illustrations by Dan Beard. 12mo. Cloth, $1.50.

"An interesting and cleverly devised book. . . . No lack of imagination. . . . Shows a skillful and wide acquaintance with scientific facts."—*New York Herald.*

"The author speculates cleverly and daringly on the scientific advance of the earth, and he revels in the physical luxuriance of Jupiter; but he also lets his imagination travel through spiritual realms, and evidently delights in mystic speculation quite as much as in scientific investigation. If he is a follower of Jules Verne, he has not forgotten also to study the philosophers."—*New York Tribune.*

"A beautiful example of typographical art and the bookmaker's skill. . . . To appreciate the story one must read it."—*New York Commercial Advertiser.*

"The date of the events narrated in this book is supposed to be 2000 A. D. The inhabitants of North America have increased mightily in numbers and power and knowledge. It is an age of marvelous scientific attainments. Flying machines have long been in common use, and finally a new power is discovered called 'apergy,' the reverse of gravitation, by which people are able to fly off into space in any direction, and at what speed they please."—*New York Sun.*

"The scientific romance by John Jacob Astor is more than likely to secure a distinct popular success, and achieve widespread vogue both as an amusing and interesting story, and a thoughtful endeavor to prophesy some of the triumphs which science is destined to win by the year 2000. The book has been written with a purpose, and that a higher one than the mere spinning of a highly imaginative yarn. Mr. Astor has been engaged upon the book for over two years, and has brought to bear upon it a great deal of hard work in the way of scientific research, of which he has been very fond ever since he entered Harvard. It is admirably illustrated by Dan Beard."—*Mail and Express.*

"Mr. Astor has himself almost all the qualities imaginable for making the science of astronomy popular. He knows the learned maps of the astrologers. He knows the work of Copernicus. He has made calculations and observations. He is enthusiastic, and the spectacular does not frighten him."—*New York Times.*

"The work will remind the reader very much of Jules Verne in its general plan of using scientific facts and speculation as a skeleton on which to hang the romantic adventures of the central figures, who have all the daring ingenuity and luck of Mr. Verne's heroes. Mr. Astor uses history to point out what in his opinion science may be expected to accomplish. It is a romance with a purpose."—*Chicago Inter-Ocean.*

"The romance contains many new and striking developments of the possibilities of science hereafter to be explored, but the volume is intensely interesting, both as a product of imagination and an illustration of the ingenious and original application of science."—*Rochester Herald.*

www.ingramcontent.com/pod-product-compliance
Lightning Source LLC
Chambersburg PA
CBHW030911270326
41929CB00008B/659